VAX/VMS

Mastering DCL Commands and Utilities

Books from QED

Database

Building the Data Warehouse
Migrating to DB2
DB2: The Complete Guide to Implementation and Use
DB2 Design Review Guidelines
DB2: Maximizing Performance of Online Production Systems
Embedded SQL for DB2
SQL for DB2 and SQL/DS Application Developers
Using DB2 to Build Decision Support Systems
Logical Data Base Design
Entity-Relationship Approach to Logical Database Design
Database Management Systems
Database Machines and Decision Support Systems
IMS Design and Implementation Techniques
Repository Manager/MVS
How to Use ORACLE SQL*PLUS
ORACLE: Building High Performance Online Systems
ORACLE Design Review Guidelines
Using ORACLE to Build Decision Support Systems
Understanding Data Pattern Processing
Developing Client/Server Applications in an Architected Environment

Systems Engineering

Information Systems Architecture in the 90's
Quality Assurance for Information Systems
The User-Interface Screen Design Handbook
Managing Software Projects
The Complete Guide to Software Testing
A User's Guide for Defining Software Requirements
A Structured Approach to Systems Testing
Rapid Application Prototyping: A New Approach to User Requirements Analysis
The Software Factory
Data Architecture
Advanced Topics in Information Engineering
Software Engineering with Formal Metrics

Management

Introduction to Data Security and Controls
How to Automate Your Computer Center: Achieving Unattended Operations

Management (cont'd)

Controlling the Future
The UNIX Industry Ethical Conflicts in Information and Computer Science, Technology, and Business
Mind Your Business

Data Communications

Designing and Implementing Ethernet Networks
Network Concepts and Architectures
Open Systems

IBM Mainframe Series

CICS/VS: A Guide to Application Debugging
CICS Application and System Programming: Tools and Techniques
CICS: A Guide To Performance Tuning
MVS COBOL II Power Programmer's Desk Reference
VSE JCL and Subroutines for Application Programmers
VSE COBOL II Power Programmer's Desk Reference
The MVS Primer
TSO/E CLISTs: The Complete Tutorial and Desk Reference
QMF: How to Use Query Management Facility with DB2 and SQL/DS
DOS/VSE: Introduction to the Operating System
DOS/VSE JCL: Mastering Job Control Language
DOS/VSE: CICS Systems Programming
DOS/VSE/SP Guide for Systems Programming
Advanced VSE System Programming Techniques
Systems Programmer's Problem Solver
VSAM: Guide to Optimization and Design
MVS/JCL: Mastering Job Control Language
MVS/TSO: Mastering CLISTs
MVS/TSO: Mastering Native Mode and ISPF
REXX in the TSO Environment

Programming

C Language for Programmers
VAX/VMS: Mastering DCL Commands and Utilities
The PC Data Handbook
UNIX C Shell Desk Reference

VAX/VMS

Mastering DCL Commands and Utilities

Daniel A. Sideris

QED Information Sciences, Inc.
Wellesley, Massachusetts

Library of Congress Catalog Number: 89-24262
International Standard Book Number 0-89435-317-9
Printed in the United States of America
        92 10 9 8 7 6 5 4

Library of Congress Cataloging-in-Publication Data

Sideris, Daniel A.
    VAX/VMS : mastering DCL commands and utilities / Daniel A. Sideris
        p.   cm.
        ISBN 0-89435-317-9
        1. VAX/VMS (Computer operating system)   I. Title.
QA76.76.063S556 1990
005.4'449--dc20

Contents

Chapter Three - File Maintenance Commands

Chapter Four - Directories

Chapter Five - File Protection and Control

Chapter Six - Logical Names and Symbols

Chapter Seven - Print and Batch Queues

Chapter Eight - EVE Editor

Chapter Nine - Mail and Phone

Preface

The purpose of this book is to provide a tutorial in using the Digital Command Language (DCL) with its numerous commands and utilities. DCL is the user interface to the VMS operating system for Digital Equipment Corporation's VAX series of computer systems.

It is hoped that this tutorial textbook may be able to fill several useful roles for those wishing to learn the fundamentals of DCL. More experienced computer users will likely find the book quite adequate as a self-study tutorial. The book may also be used as a textbook for undergraduate-level courses in computer operating systems or the VAX/VMS operating system in particular. And, finally, the book may be used for lecture notes and student textbooks as part of instructor-led training seminars within the field of commercial business.

The Digital Command Language, introduced in the late-1970s with the release of the first VAX/VMS computer systems, proved to be quite revolutionary in its structure. While offering fairly sophisticated features, its greatest and perhaps most noticeable feature is the relative simplicity of its format and its ease-of-use, something quite remarkable for a computer operating system's command language. For perhaps the first time, this opened up to non-technical end-users the ability to use the command language interface to a computer operating system. Shortly after the introduction of DCL and the VAX/VMS operating system, the computer industry would be revolutionized throughout the 1980s with the introduction of personal computers and "end-user" computing. Such phrases as "human engineering" and "user-friendly computing" quickly became the rage, at least in rhetoric, if not always in fact. In any event, by providing such a user-friendly command language for its mid-range VAX computer systems, Digital proved to be quite visionary in its design of DCL.

As the VAX computer line has matured and expanded over the past several years, Digital has carried the DCL language over to all VAX/VMS platforms. As the first chapter within this book explains, VAX/VMS systems now include desktop, single-user and low-end systems, such as the VAXstation and MicroVAX systems, mid-range systems, such as the original 700 series and the newer 8000 and 6000 series, and finally the introduction of the new mainframe 9000 series of VAX systems. In all cases, the VAX/VMS operating system and its DCL interface have been uniformly applied across all of these platforms. Thus, computer users who learn the DCL interface to the VAX/VMS operating system can now utilize their expertise in using the entire line of VAX systems, from the desktop VAXstations to the mainframe 9000 series.

Aside from the appeal to non-technical end-users, Digital's decision to construct such a "user-friendly" command language has been quite instrumental in the success and acceptance of the VAX/VMS computer line within the laboratories and corporate data centers of the commercial business world. Even among seasoned computer professionals, long accustomed to dealing with complex command languages and computer systems, there has been a desire for more consistency, structure and simplicity, thereby allowing efforts to be focused on using computers to solve truly complex technical problems, rather than having to expend time and energies dealing with the peculiarities of the computer system itself.

In determining what the focus of this book should be, we have taken a que from Digital and attempted to follow the style of DCL itself. Our main goal is to present the information in as simple and logical a manner as possible, while preserving the technical facts and other key details. This book is not meant to serve as a replacement to the technical manuals provided with the VAX/VMS operating system by Digital, which record each and every possible "twist-and-turn" of DCL. Rather, it provides an easy-to-read, pleasant guide into the many features of DCL while sometimes, in the interests of simplicity, leaving out the more esoteric or rarely used options.

The chapters within the book proceed from the simpler to the more involved aspects of DCL. The introductory information within chapter one allows users to log on to a VAX system and become familiar with the different types of terminal connections that may exist within their system configuration. Chapter two discusses basic commands that allow users to tailor the DCL environment to their preferences, a feature of DCL that adds considerably to its ease of use.

Chapters three through five deal primarily with DCL files. Chapter three considers the commands necessary to create, modify, delete, etc., the files users require. Chapter four discusses VMS "directories" or the areas of storage used to contain DCL files. And chapter five explains the various methods of restricting access to the information contained within these files.

Chapter six considers a very sophisticated feature of VMS and DCL, namely logical names and symbols. These may be considered among the more complicated options available within DCL. The chapter presents the basics of logical names and symbols and will provide a base of information on these topics that seasoned computer professionals can use later.

Chapter seven discusses background processing within VMS by means of print and batch queues.

Chapters eight and nine present the very popular DCL utilities EVE, MAIL and PHONE.

Each of the chapters includes workshop exercises that the reader may attempt on their own VAX/VMS system. Possible answers to these exercises (sometimes there are several) are listed after the exercises in a separate "answer section".

One last brief note regarding the content and approach should be mentioned, pertaining to command procedures. Command procedures are only briefly considered within the textbook. This feature is probably the most sophisticated of all of those available within DCL, allowing computer programmers and other technical computer professionals to actually implement complex logic and complete programs within DCL command procedures.

Chapter One

Introduction

VAX/VMS Overview

The VAX family of computers is, today, one of the most successful computer systems ever developed. VAX systems are now used in virtually every business environment and may be found in nearly every developed nation in the world. The success of the VAX/VMS architecture, together with its DECnet networking features, is perhaps the single largest factor in the spectacular growth during recent years of Digital Equipment Corporation, the manufacturer of the VAX. Today, Digital Equipment Corporation (DEC) is the second largest computer manufacturer in the world, second only to IBM, and the VAX family of computers is the most successful mid-range computer system from any manufacturer.

In the late 1970s, DEC released the first series of VAX hardware systems, the 700 series. The Virtual Address Extension (VAX) system was a successor to another popular hardware system produced by DEC, the PDP-11. The VMS (Virtual Memory System) operating system was released simultaneously as the software environment for the VAX. Although VAX systems also support DEC's version of UNIX as an alternate operating system, the majority of VAX systems as of this writing employ VMS as the operating system.

To a large extent, the tremendous success of the VAX architecture has been due to the VMS operating system, as opposed to the specific merits of the hardware. Many people acknowledge VMS as one of the most sophisticated operating systems ever developed, and it is certainly one of the most popular.

The popularity of VMS has been especially enhanced in that it is uniformly applied over all the VAX hardware series. In the years following the introduction of the VAX and the initial 700 series models, DEC has produced several newer VAX series which incorporate the advances available in computer hardware technology. Today VAX systems run the spectrum from the MicroVAX line that sells for as little as a few thousand dollars in some configurations to the mid-range 6000 and 8000 line that can sell for hundreds of thousands of dollars, on up to the newer 9000 mainframe series with a cost in the millions of dollars. However, in all cases, the VMS operating system is uniformly applied over all VAX models within each of the VAX series.

Thus, users of the VMS software environment need not be concerned with which

VAX series or model they are using, as the commands, utilities and software programs are completely transportable and executable on any VAX system.

For the remainder of this first chapter, we will consider the following topics:

- Overview information regarding the Digital Command Language (DCL) interface to the VMS operating system.

- The process of logging on and off a VAX/VMS system.

- The VMS file specification and file specification wildcards.

- The VMS HELP utility.

At the end of this chapter, as well as each remaining chapter within the book, exercises have been prepared to allow you to try the functions described.

Digital Command Language

Strictly speaking, a user of the VAX/VMS operating system does not interact directly with VMS, but rather, uses the Digital Command Language (DCL) as an interface to the operating system. A large part of the aforementioned popularity of the VMS operating system is attributable to the DCL interface to VMS, which is both simple and very powerful. The transportability of VMS software across all the VAX hardware models also applies to the DCL interface.

Readers who are learning DCL as their first command language should be able to become fairly proficient within a short period of time. Those readers who are familiar with other command languages will likely find DCL to be conceptually similar to what you already know. Functions and tasks which you are used to performing in other environments can also be performed with DCL, and oftentimes more easily and in a logical fashion.

As an example of the simplicity of the DCL interface, many of the commands are quite intuitive, even to the point of being obvious. For instance, if a user needed to print a document on a printer attached to the VAX, the DCL command for this function is PRINT. If one would like to type the contents of the document out on the terminal screen, the command is TYPE. Or if there is the need to delete a file from the disk storage device, the command is DELETE, and so on. Thus, while unfortunately there are some exceptions, the DCL interface is generally quite logical, consistent and easy to use.

Login Process

In order to prevent unauthorized use of a computer system, nearly all operating systems, including VMS, require that a user supply a user identification name (known as a user name in VMS) and a matching password, as assigned by the system manager, prior to allowing the user to perform any work or access any data. This process is known as *logging in.*

The login process will vary depending upon how a terminal is connected to a VAX host. The two most common connection methods are listed as follows and the login process for each will be considered within this chapter.

1)   A direct, local connection from the terminal device to a terminal controller port on a single VAX system. This may also be referred to as a "hard-wired" connection.

2)   The terminal is connected to an Ethernet terminal server, which has the ability to connect to as many as several dozen or even hundreds of different VAX host systems within an Ethernet local area network.

The simplest method of logging in is available when the user terminal is directly connected, or "hard-wired," to a single VAX host. In this case, the user need only follow the steps listed below:

•   Power on the user terminal and press the RETURN key when the terminal has completed any self-tests and is ready.

•   Read the announcement message, if any, that may have been established by the system manager and that is displayed on the terminal screen.

•   The VAX system will prompt for a user name, as assigned by the system manager. The user must enter the assigned user name and press RETURN. It does not matter if the entry is upper or lower case.

•   The system will next prompt for a password for the user name. The password is initially assigned by the system manager but may be changed thereafter by the user. After entering the password the user must press RETURN. If the user name/password combination is entered incorrectly, an error message will be displayed and you must try again.

•   For security reasons the system manager may require a second

password to be entered. If this has been done for the user name, the
VAX will prompt the user for the second password. The second
password entry must also be terminated with the RETURN key.

Once again, for security reasons, the password(s) that you type in is not echoed
back or displayed on the terminal screen as it is entered. While this requires you
to type carefully in order to avoid any typing errors, it also prevents someone
from stealing your password by watching the password entry and then being able
to later gain access to your system and your data.

Note the following sample login process using the example user name of
SMITH. Note that this particular user name requires the entry of only a single
password. Also, note that although the password is entered by the user and
terminated with the RETURN key, no characters are echoed on the terminal
screen.

```
VAX Host System SI860B

Username: SMITH
Password:

        Welcome to VAX/VMS version V5.1-1 on node SI860B
     Last interactive login on Wednesday, 19-JUL-1989 21:00
   Last non-interactive login on Wednesday, 19-JUL-1989 10:00

$
```

If you wait too long to enter the user name and password, or if you enter a
wrong combination, your login attempt is rejected. Simply press the RETURN
key, though, and you will again be prompted for a user name/password
combination.

Once a user has correctly entered a valid user name/password combination, VMS
creates an interactive process. All activity by the user will be conducted within
the control of this process, or perhaps sub-processes that the user may also
create. The process first displays various system status messages and may
execute initialization procedures to set up the process. The dollar sign prompt ($)
is then displayed and indicates that the user's interactive process has been created
and set up, that the process is at DCL level and the user may now enter DCL
commands.

When the user logs off of the system, the interactive process, along with any
sub-processes created, is deleted. The time period between logon and logoff,

during which the user's process is active, is known as a *session*. Thus, a user may have several sessions throughout the day or perhaps only one session.

Ethernet Login

While the above login process for "hard-wired" terminals is the simplest, it is also limited. Since the user terminal is directly connected to a single VAX, the user either cannot access other VAX systems or must do so using the original VAX host as a "router," which is not always very efficient.

With the tremendous popularity of Ethernet local area networking over recent years, a more common and more functional terminal connection is for terminals to be connected to an Ethernet terminal server, rather than a specific VAX system. While logging in with such a terminal connection is slightly more complicated, you have direct access to all VAX systems within your corporate local area network and not just a single system.

When connected to an Ethernet terminal server, the following differences will exist in the login process:

• When the terminal is first powered on, the announcement message displayed is from the terminal server, and not from any particular VAX host system.

• The user must first log on to the terminal server.

• The user must next indicate to the terminal server which of several available VAX systems is requested.

• The VAX system indicated will then respond with its individual system announcement message, user name prompt and password prompts, as described already.

The following sample screen shows the announcement message from the terminal server and the user login to the terminal server system.

```
DECserver 500 Terminal Server  V1.1 - LAT V5.1

Please type HELP if you need assistance

Enter username> anyname
Local>
```

Remember that the initial request for a user name as shown above is **not** a VMS user name for a particular VAX system. It is a terminal server user name that is required to login to the terminal server system. The user name entered is not validated or verified in any way, however. While you must generally enter something, any name entered is accepted.

The "Local> " prompt indicates that the user has successfully logged in to the terminal server. At this point, only terminal server commands may be entered. DCL commands are not allowed and you are not yet connected to any VAX/VMS system.

With so many different VAX systems available to you from the terminal server, before you can supply a valid user name/password combination for a specific VAX system, you must inform the terminal server of which VAX system you wish to access. This is done with the terminal server CONNECT command. The system or network manager can inform you of the names of the VAX systems to which you can connect. Or, you may use the terminal server SHOW SERVICES command to list the available VAX systems:

```
Local> SHOW SERVICES

Service Name        Status          Identification

SI860A              Available       General Ledger VAX
SI860B              3 Connected     Accounts Payable VAX
SI860C              Available       Accounts Payable VAX

Local>
```

Note
VAX systems are identified by terminal servers as "services." An Ethernet "service" may actually be a cluster of VAX systems, although such a VAXcluster will appear as a single system to users.

Once we have determined the VAX system or "service" that we wish to access, we may use the terminal server CONNECT command to connect to the desired service, which in our example is SI860B. Once we have connected to a valid VAX system within the Ethernet local area network, the VAX responds to our login request in the same manner as to a "hard-wired" terminal. A valid user name/password combination must be entered allowing VMS to create an interactive process for the user and to place the user process at DCL command level. Note the following example.

```
Local> CONNECT SI860B
Local -010- Session 1 to SI860B established



Username: SMITH
Password:
```

In order to simplify the login process for users connected to a terminal server, the terminal server manager may modify the environment in many different ways, such as the following:

- When the user terminal is powered on, a terminal server user name is automatically assigned by the terminal server manager and the user automatically placed at the "Local>" prompt.

- The user may enter the terminal server CONNECT command without listing or selecting a specific service. A default or preferred service for the user is automatically used and the preferred VAX host system responds with the system announcement message and the user name/password prompt.

There may be other differences as well, depending upon the customization options used at your site. If you have any problems connecting and logging in to your desired VAX host system, consult with your network or system manager for the specific configuration that you have.

Once again, when the DCL prompt ($) is displayed, the user may enter any DCL command or utility, as we will consider throughout the textbook.

Logout Process

Once a user has completed a session of DCL activity and wishes to terminate the session and the VMS process, the user must log out. When the user enters the LOGOUT command, the following steps are performed:

- The system displays either a brief or full logout message.

- The interactive process created for the user at the time of login is deleted. If the terminal is connected to a terminal server, the terminal server "Local>" prompt is again displayed.

- The user's session is completed and the user must log in once again in order to gain access to the VAX and DCL command level.

Note the use of the DCL command to logout for a user terminal connected via a terminal server. A brief logout message is displayed by default.

```
$ LOGOUT
    SMITH          logged out at 28-JUL-1989 09:39:23.47
```

The next example shows a logout with a full logout message, listing various statistics regarding the interactive session just completed.

```
$ LOGOUT/FULL
    SMITH          logged out at 28-JUL-1989 09:39:56.34

    Accounting information:
    Buffered I/O count:        55      Peak working set size:     429
    Direct I/O count:          25      Peak page file size:       924
    Page faults:              378      Mounted volumes:             0
    Charged CPU time:    0 00:00:01.97 Elapsed time:      0 00:00:10.03
```

If the terminal was hard-wired to the VAX host system, the user may invoke the login function once again by simply pressing the RETURN key at a later time.

If the terminal was connected to a terminal server, the logout function returns the user back to the "Local>" prompt and the terminal server command level. At the terminal server command level, the following options are available:

- The user may invoke the login process on the same VAX at a later time by entering the CONNECT command.

- The user may login to another VAX by naming the other VAX system with the CONNECT command.

- The user may enter any other terminal server command, such as SHOW SERVICES or many others not considered within the textbook.

- The user may log off the terminal server.

The following example shows a user at the terminal server command level logging off the terminal server.

```
Local> LOGOUT
local -010- logged of port 115
```

Note

Remember that only terminal server commands may be entered from the terminal server "Local> " prompt, not DCL commands. It is simply coincidental that the logout command happens to be identical for both the terminal server and DCL.

VMS File Specification

Before we consider any additional DCL commands or utilities, we will first give attention to the subject of the VMS file specification. One of the most fundamental requirements of using the VAX/VMS operating system and its DCL interface is an understanding of this specification. While there are certainly exceptions, a great majority of the DCL commands you are most likely to use each day will require a file specification.

For example, if one is going to PRINT a document or other data, the information is stored by VMS within a file and must be identified according to the rules for VMS files. If one is going to DELETE a document, once again the file to be deleted must be specified, and so on.

File names are comprised of two basic components, (1) the file name itself, and (2) a file name extension. Note the following command to print a memo document created with one of the VMS editors:

```
           1       2

$ PRINT FILE1.MEMO
```

Some of the rules for a file name and its extension that you will want to remember are as follows:

- The file name may include an underscore (_), hyphen (-) or a dollar sign ($), but most other special characters are illegal.

- The file name may be a maximum of 39 characters in length.

- The file name and its extension must be separated by a period.

- The file name extension may be a maximum of 39 characters in length.

- When initially creating and naming a file, the file name extension is optional.

As you will no doubt come to appreciate the more you work with VAX systems, they are typically very interconnected via a number of networking options. (This is actually a fundamental part of Digital's overall distributed computing strategy.) More often than not, the VAX system that you will work with will not be a stand-alone system, but rather will be part of a network of VAXs maintained by your company.

As a result of this connectivity or networking, the data or files which you need to access may not be stored on your local VAX. And even if the file is located on your local system, it may not be contained within your personal directory of files. Therefore, simply identifying a file with its name and extension is sometimes insufficient for VMS to locate a file.

Hence, the following additional components of a VMS file specification may also be required:

- Network node (system) name

- Device (disk or magnetic tape) specification

- User directory (account) specification

As stated, the file you wish to access may be stored on any number of VAX systems. Hence, the node name identifies to VMS which VAX system within the network contains the file. Once an individual VAX system has been identified, there are a number of data storage devices, typically disks and tapes. The next step, then, is to identify via the device name, which of these devices on the designated VAX contains the data file. Finally, a single storage device may contain directories for any number of users, so you must include a directory name.

Directories are private areas of storage on a disk device which are reserved for a single user or group of users for storage of their personal data files. A private directory for a user may further be divided up into subsidiary subdirectories. Both directories and subdirectories are considered in greater detail in a later chapter.

Note the following complete file specifications below, where the node name, device name and directory name are used:

```
     1        2        3        4

SI860B::DUA0:[SMITH]FILE1.MEMO

SI860A::DUA2:[JONES]SAMPLE_FILE.DATA
```

The following syntax rules apply to a full VMS file specification:

1) The node name, assigned by the network or system manager, must be the first component of the file specification, followed by a double colon (::).

2) The device name must follow the node name, and contain a single colon (:) as a suffix.

3) The directory name must follow the device name and be enclosed in square brackets ([ ]).

4) The file name follows. Note there are no spaces allowed between the various components of the file specification.

Note

Although we may use the file specification rules discussed to identify a file on another VAX system or in another user's directory, this does not necessarily mean that we have been authorized to access the file. This is determined by VMS file security, which is considered in a later chapter. The VMS file specification only identifies the file, but the user's access is still subject to the VMS checks for security.

When a DCL user modifies a VMS file, as with an editor or other utility, in most cases the file is not actually changed. Rather, a new version of the file is created, which contains the modifications, while the original file, under an earlier version number, remains intact. This provides the obvious advantage to the user of reviewing older versions of a file or perhaps accessing an older version to roll back changes that have been made.

The first time a file is created, it is assigned a version number of one (1). If it is modified, the modified file is assigned a version number of two (2), and so on. The version number of a file is specified after the other components of the file specification and is prefaced with a semicolon (;).

The example below demonstrates the complete VMS file specification, with all its possible options, including the version number.

```
SI860B::DUA0:[SMITH]USER_FILE_ONE.MEMO;4
```

As one looks at the example of the complete file specification, you might imagine that it would be quite tedious to type all the components of the specification each time you need to access a file. VMS alleviates this problem by providing default values according to the following rules:

- If the node name component is omitted, your local VAX system is assumed.

- If the device and directory name are omitted, the default device and directory are assumed. We will consider later how to set a default device and directory for your process or session.

- If the version number is omitted, the most recent version is assumed.

As you will no doubt agree, the majority of the files that you will access will likely be located on your local VAX system and in your personal, default device and directory. And the majority of the time that you will access these files, you will want the most recent version. Therefore, most times, simply stating the file name and its extension, as shown in the original example of this section, is sufficient to identify a file.

File Specification Wildcards

We have just seen the syntax of the VMS file specification that allows a user to access his or her own data files, as well as data that may reside within another user's directory, another storage device, or even another VAX within the network (subject, of course, to security privileges).

It is often necessary, though, to access several files within these locations as a group, based upon a common storage location, common elements within the file name or extension, etc. This is provided within DCL by means of *wildcards*.

For example, suppose that you would like to print out all four memos that are stored within your personal directory. This could be accomplished by entering four separate DCL PRINT commands and the file name of the four memo files, as follows:

```
$ PRINT FILE1.MEMO
$ PRINT FILE2.MEMO
$ PRINT FILE3.MEMO
$ PRINT FILE4.MEMO
```

The tedium of executing the same command separately for each file increases as the number of files desired increases. Obviously, there must be a better way, especially when we note that each file happens to contain the same file name extension of .MEMO. With the asterisk (*) wildcard, we could perform the above function with a single command, selecting all files that end in a file name extension of .MEMO and using the wildcard as a placeholder for any characters that may exist in the file name:

```
$ PRINT *.MEMO
```

Thus, any file that has been assigned a file name extension of .MEMO is selected for printing with only a single PRINT command.

The wildcard may be used anywhere within the file name or file name extension. Perhaps we have a number of files pertaining to an Accounts Payable project, named ACCOUNTS_PAYABLE.MEMO, ACCOUNTS_PAYABLE.REPORT, and so on. We could select all Accounts Payable files for printing with the command:

```
$ PRINT ACCOUNTS_PAYABLE.*
```

Wildcards may also be used to represent a portion of the file name or extension. The next example selects files that contain the characters "WEEK" somewhere within the file name, but not necessarily at the beginning or end, and the characters "MEMO" somewhere within the file name extension.

```
$ PRINT *WEEK*.*MEMO*
```

Whether or not wildcards are used, the rule regarding version numbers remains the same. Unless a specific version number is specified, only the most recent version of each file is selected. The asterisk wildcard may be used in the version number component of the file specification to indicate all versions of a file.

```
$ PRINT *WEEK*.*MEMO*;*
```

The asterisk wildcard may also be used within the directory portion of the file specification, to select files within all directories that match the characters supplied. As an example, suppose you wanted to print all versions of all .MEMO files within all user directories that contained the prefix AP (for directories associated with the Accounts Payable project, such as [AP_SMITH], [AP_JONES], [CONTROL_AP], and so on). The following command will search through all user directories on the default disk device that contain the characters "AP" somewhere within the directory name, and select all files therein that have a file name extension of ".MEMO". Additionally, all versions of those files are selected.

```
$ PRINT [*AP*]*.MEMO;*
```

Note

In order for the wildcard feature to be useful, it requires the user to use forethought when initially assigning file names at the time the file is created. If the user had not used a file name extension of ".MEMO" for all the memo files created, the above examples would not have been possible. Thus, while VMS imposes no restrictions on the specific file names or extensions that a user may select, judicious assignment of these names will allow for wildcards to be used at a later date to select these files.

The percent sign (%) wildcard performs a function similar to the asterisk with the exception that it holds the place of one and only one character.

Assuming that we had memo files named FILE1.MEMO, FILE2.MEMO through FILE99.MEMO, the first wildcard specification shown below would select only FILE1.MEMO through FILE9.MEMO, ignoring any files with more than one character after the initial characters "FILE" in the name. The second example would select files FILE1.MEMO through FILE99.MEMO by means of the two percent sign (%) wildcards. (Both examples indicate only the most recent file version).

```
$ PRINT FILE%.MEMO

$ PRINT FILE%%.MEMO
```

Finally, several wildcards may be included within a single file specification to very selectively access a group of files. The following example searches all user directories on the current default device and selects all versions of all memo files that include the characters WEEK at the beginning of the file name, followed by any one character:

```
$ PRINT [*]WEEK%.MEMO;*
```

As a concluding example of wildcards, the following command would print all versions of all files in all the main user directories contained on the disk device DUA0 of the VAX host system SI860B.

```
$ PRINT SI860B::DUA0:[*]*.*;*
```

HELP

The first DCL utility that we will consider is the one that is most helpful as a tutorial to new users and as a reference for experienced users, namely the VMS HELP utility.

The HELP utility provides a quick, on-line reference manual for all DCL commands and utilities, as well as additional system information. By simply entering the HELP command at the DCL dollar sign ($) prompt, users may run the utility and specify the information desired.

While at DCL command level, the HELP command invokes the utility and displays introductory information regarding the use of HELP. Notice the following example, where the user has invoked the utility and receives a display of the introductory page.

HELP

The HELP command invokes the VAX-11 HELP Facility to display information about a VMS command or topic. In response to the "Topic?" prompt, you can:

Type the name of the command or topic for which you need help.

Type PROCEDURES for information on commonly peformed tasks.

Type HINTS if you are not sure of the name of the command or topic for which you need help.

Type INSTRUCTIONS for more detailed instructions on how to use HELP.

Type a question mark (?) to redisplay the most recently requested text.

Press the RETURN key one or more times to exit from HELP.

You can abbreviate any topic name, although ambiguous abbreviations result

Press RETURN to continue ...

By pressing the RETURN key as instructed, the utility lists the first section of DCL commands and utilities. Note the following display:

```
Format:
 HELP [topic[subtopic]...]


Additional information available:

ACCOUNTING ALLOCATE   ANALYZE      APPEND     Ascii        ASSIGN       ATTACH
BACKUP     BASIC      CALL         CANCEL     CLOSE        Command_procedure
CONNECT    CONTINUE   CONVERT      COPY       CREATE       DEALLOCATE DEASSIGN
DEBUG      DECK       DEFINE       DELETE     DEPOSIT      DIFFERENCES
DIRECTORY  DISCONNECT DISMOUNT     DUMP       EDIT         EOD          EXAMINE
EXIT       Expressions             File_spec  GOSUB        GOTO         HELP
Hints      IF         INITIALIZE   INQUIRE    Instructions              Lexicals
LIBRARY    LINK       LOGOUT       MAIL       MERGE        MESSAGE      MOUNT
New_Features_V44      Numbers      ON         OPEN         PRINT
Privileges Procedures Protection   PURGE      READ         RECALL       RENAME
REPLY      REQUEST    RETURN       RUN        RUNOFF       SEARCH       SET


Press RETURN to continue ...
```

Pressing the RETURN key a second time lists the second and last section of DCL commands and utilities for which help is available.

Once the list of topics is displayed, the user may enter a topic for which help is desired. Once the overview information for the topic is listed, the user has the following options:

- Selecting information regarding a subtopic, that is, specific details for the topic, by entering one of the subtopic names listed.

- Entering a question mark (?) to re-display the list of available topics or subtopics.

- Entering an asterisk (*) to display detailed information for all the subtopics.

- Pressing the RETURN key to exit the subtopic level and return to the topic level within HELP. Pressing the RETURN key at the topic level returns the user back to DCL level.

The example below shows the subtopics available for the LOGOUT topic. You will notice that detailed information is available regarding the /FULL option, as well as others, for the LOGOUT command.

```
LOGOUT

  Terminates a terminal session.

  Format
   LOGOUT


  Additional information available:

  Qualifiers
   /BRIEF (default)        /FULL        /HANGUP

LOGOUT Subtopic?
```

Chapter One Exercises

In order to perform the exercises for this first chapter, as well as all subsequent chapters, you must first do the following:

- Obtain from the system manager a valid user name/password for your system.

- For terminals connected to a terminal server within an Ethernet local area network, obtain from either the system manager or the network manager the name of the Ethernet service that identifies the VAX host system on which the user name/password has been established.

Exercise 1
Hard-Wired Terminals

a) Power on the terminal and press the RETURN key to display the system announcement message (if any) and receive the VAX user name prompt.

b) Establish an interactive session by entering the user name/password combination you have been given and note the status messages and dollar sign prompt indicating that you have successfully created a VMS process and are at the DCL command level.

c) Terminate the interactive session by entering the LOGOUT command.

d) Log in once again and establish a second interactive session. Terminate this session by entering the LOGOUT/FULL command and viewing the display of process statistics.

Exercise 2
Ethernet Terminals

a) Power on the terminal and press the RETURN key to receive the terminal server user name prompt and enter any desired user name and press RETURN.

b) Enter the terminal server command SHOW SERVICES and look for the service name for your VAX system.

c) Using the service name, connect to your VAX system using the CONNECT command.

d) Establish an interactive session by entering the user name/password combination you have been given in response to the prompts from the VAX host system.

e) Terminate the interactive session by entering the LOGOUT command.

f) Log in once again to establish a second interactive session. Terminate this session by entering the LOGOUT/FULL command and viewing the process statistics.

g) When at the terminal server "Local> " prompt, log off the terminal server with the LOGOUT command.

Exercise 3
All Users

From DCL command level (the dollar sign prompt), invoke the HELP utility for information regarding the topics and subtopics available.

a) Enter the HELP command.

b) View the introduction screen and the list of topics by pressing the RETURN key when indicated.

c) While viewing the list of help topics, select the following topics by entering them in response to the help prompt.

- LOGOUT
- Instructions

d) When viewing the LOGOUT topic, select help regarding the /FULL subtopic or enter the asterisk (*) for help on all subtopics for LOGOUT.

Exercise Answers

Not applicable for the exercises within this chapter.

Chapter Two

Basic Commands

Overview

This chapter introduces you to a number of fairly simple DCL commands. These commands perform basic operations that you may need to display the status of various conditions, customize the DCL environment to your personal preference, and other functions.

The SET command has several options that permit the user to customize the DCL environment. The options of the SET command considered within this chapter are as follows:

- SET PROMPT
- SET PROCESS/NAME
- SET PASSWORD
- SET CONTROL
- SET BROADCAST
- SET TERMINAL

The SHOW command displays the status of various items for a user process or the system. Many of the items that are changed with the SET command may be displayed with the SHOW command. Options that we will consider with the SHOW command are as follows:

- SHOW TIME
- SHOW USERS
- SHOW SYSTEM
- SHOW QUOTA
- SHOW PROCESS
- SHOW BROADCAST
- SHOW TERMINAL

In addition to the SET and SHOW commands, we will also consider:

- RECALL command
- An introduction to DCL command procedures

SET PROMPT

One of several customization features provided within DCL is the SET PROMPT command. This command allows the user to change the DCL prompt from the dollar sign ($), the default, to a prompt of the user's choice.

This may be done as follows:

```
$ SET PROMPT="New prompt> "
New prompt>
```

Changing the prompt does not affect any function or operation within DCL. The same DCL commands and utilities are entered from the new prompt just as with the default dollar sign prompt. The only effect is that the user has customized the prompt to be displayed.

The effect of the changed prompt is temporary, only for the current process or session. After the user logs off and back on again, the default dollar sign prompt is used for the new session. The default prompt may also be restored by using the SET PROMPT command without specifying any new prompt string.

```
New prompt> SET PROMPT
$
```

There is obviously little consequence to changing the default DCL prompt apart from personal preference, and at first this may seem to be a rather useless command. There are several cases, though, where this command may prove quite helpful.

Some users may have user accounts available to them from several different VAXs and use several of the different VAX hosts throughout the day by means of the terminal server connections. Such users may find it helpful to change the prompt for a process to be the VAX system or node name. Thus, as the user is working at DCL command level and viewing the node name as the prompt, it is immediately obvious which VAX host is being used at the moment.

SET PROCESS/NAME

All interactive users on the system, along with non-interactive system jobs and batch jobs, operate within the environment of their respective process. Whenever a new process is created, such as when a user logs in and an interactive process is created, the process is assigned a process identification number (PID) and a process name.

The PID is a random number that is automatically generated by the system and serves as a unique identification of a particular process. The process name also serves a similar purpose in that it serves as an alphabetic label that distinguishes one process from another. There are several options of the SHOW command that we will consider later within this chapter that display the current list of processes on the system, listing the PID and the process name of each process.

By default, the alphabetic name that is assigned to a process is generally either the user name specified during the time of login or the terminal line number to which the user is connected. This is the name that is listed for your process when you or other users enter the SHOW command to display current processes.

The default name assigned to your process may not be descriptive enough for you or others to identify your process. Therefore, as another of the customization features of DCL, users are permitted to select and assign a different alphabetic name for the process.

As an example, the following command changes the default process name for SMITH to include his telephone number extension. The new process name will then be visible to other users with options of the SHOW command.

```
$ SET PROCESS/NAME="J Smith x5522"
```

We will observe the effect of this command when we view the display generated by the SHOW PROCESS, SHOW USERS and SHOW SYSTEM commands.

Remember the following rules regarding the assignment of a customized process name:

- The name may be no more than 15 characters in length.

- Generally, you may not use a process name that is already used by another process already on the system.

- The name you assign is valid only for the current process. The next process you create, when you next log in, will receive a default process name.

SET PASSWORD

The PASSWORD option of the SET command is one of the few options available to general DCL users (as opposed to system manager users) that will permanently change the DCL environment. Unlike the other options we have considered, SET PASSWORD allows the user to alter the password for the user name account permanently or until changed by either the system manager or the user with another SET PASSWORD command.

The system manager has the option to prohibit certain users from changing their password. However, if you have been allowed this option, you may use the command whenever you feel there is a need.

For security reasons, the system manager may also assign an expiration date to your password. The first time that you log in after the expiration date has passed, you will be required to change the password. This is done to prevent the indefinite use of the same password for an account, which may present security risks.

When changing a password, the following events occur:

- The user is prompted for the entry of the existing (old) password.

- The user is next prompted for the entry of the new password.

- The user is required to enter the new password a second time in order to verify what the new password will be.

As one might expect, for security reasons none of the passwords entered by the user during this procedure are echoed back on the terminal.

Once the password has been changed, the next login that the user attempts must utilize the new password. Note the following example to change a password.

```
$ SET PASSWORD
Old password:
New password:
Verification:
```

Remember the following rules regarding the assignment of a password:

- The maximum length of a password is 31 characters.

- The system manager may establish a minimum length for a password, such as 6 characters.

- The longer and more complex your password is, the less likely that an authorized user will be able to guess the correct password and gain access to your account and data files.

SET CONTROL

There are several different DCL functions which may be invoked by pressing a control key. Within this section, we will consider two of these functions, CONTROL T and CONTROL Y.

The CONTROL T key function briefly interrupts the program or utility that you are running or executing and provides a one-line information line describing the current status of your process. An example of the information line from the CONTROL T function is shown below.

```
EARTH::SMITH 15:01:15   (DCL)   CPU=00:00:04.92 PF=916 IO=277 MEM=150
```

The information line includes the following:

- The VAX system name.
- The user name.
- The current system time.
- The current program being executed (in the example, the user was at DCL level).
- The amount of CPU time the process has used.
- Statistics regarding memory and input/output resources used by the process.

Once the information line is displayed, the program or utility that was interrupted automatically resumes from the point at which the interrupt occurred without any loss of data or any other harmful effect. You may press CONTROL T as often as you wish during the execution of a program.

The CONTROL Y key function also interrupts a currently executing program, but usually serves the purpose of stopping the execution permanently. The function immediately aborts the program or utility and returns the user to DCL command level. This key is useful if you desire to abort or terminate a program without waiting for its normal completion.

In the following example, the HELP utility is invoked and begins executing and displaying information on the screen. The CONTROL Y function interrupts the utility and returns the user immediately to DCL command level.

```
HELP

    The HELP command invokes the VAX-11 HELP Facility to display information
    about a VMS command or topic.  In response to the "Topic?" prompt, you can:

      Type the name of the command or topic for which you need help.

      Type PROCEDURES for information on commonly peformed tasks.

      Type HINTS if you are not sure of the name of the
    Interrupt

$
```

Once at DCL command level, the user may enter other DCL commands and thereby abort the utility or program that was executing. In the event that the CONTROL Y key was pressed inadvertently, the user may resume the program as long as no other program or utility was started. In the next example, immediately following the CONTROL Y interrupt, the user enters the DCL command CONTINUE and resumes processing of the HELP utility.

```
$ CONTINUE
        for which you need help.

      Type INSTRUCTIONS for more detailed instructions on how to use HELP.

      Type a question mark (?) to redisplay the most recently requested text.

      Press the RETURN key one or more times to exit from HELP.

    You can abbreviate any topic name, although ambiguous abbreviations result

Press RETURN to continue ...
```

There are several commands provided within DCL that do not start another program or utility but are known as "built-in" commands. These commands may be entered following a CONTROL Y interrupt without altering the process context. Thereafter, the CONTINUE command may still be used to resume processing of the original program. Consult the user documentation from Digital if you would like a list of the "built-in" commands that may be used in this manner.

Depending upon the initialization for processes established by the system manager, your process may or may not have the CONTROL T and Y functions active, although generally they will be active. If they are not, then pressing the keys has no effect.

You may activate or enable these keys individually or together by entering the following command:

```
$ SET CONTROL=T
$ SET CONTROL=Y

$ SET CONTROL=(T,Y)
```

Once these keys are enabled, you may disable them with the following variation of the SET CONTROL command:

```
$ SET NOCONTROL=(T,Y)
```

As with most of the commands that we consider within this chapter, the effect of SET CONTROL is temporary and affects only the current user session.

SET BROADCAST

While you are working with DCL, several different types of messages may be broadcast to one or more user terminals throughout the day by the VMS operating system. These messages are broadcast to inform one or more users of certain events of which they must be aware. One example is the information message that is broadcast when the user presses the CONTROL T key. Examples of other messages broadcast to terminals are listed below:

- Messages from the MAIL utility (considered later) informing users that they have received new mail.

- Messages from the PHONE utility (also considered later) informing users that another VMS user wishes to contact them immediately.

- Messages from the system manager regarding special events or emergencies on the system.

- Messages from other utilities or events that may occur on the system.

While it is helpful to receive these messages, they may also be annoying, particularly those that can be generated by other users who are running the MAIL or PHONE utilities. Thus, DCL provides users with the option of selecting which messages they wish and do not wish to receive. This is done with the SET BROADCAST command. For example, we could refuse any messages that would be displayed by the MAIL or PHONE utilities. Or, having refused such messages, we could later accept these once again.

```
$ SET BROADCAST=(NOMAIL, NOPHONE)

$ SET BROADCAST=(MAIL, PHONE)
```

The following list represents messages that you may wish to refuse from time to time, depending upon your current activity. Use the highlighted key word within the SET BROADCAST command to select or refuse the type of message indicated.

- **MAIL / NOMAIL**, messages generated by the MAIL utility.

- **PHONE / NOPHONE**, messages generated by the PHONE utility.

- **DCL / NODCL**, messages generated by DCL, such as those received from the CONTROL T key.

- **QUEUE / NOQUEUE**, messages pertaining to user jobs within the print or batch queues.

- **GENERAL / NOGENERAL**, general messages generated by the data center operators or by the system manager.

The following list represents messages that you should not refuse. While you have the option to do so, these messages inform users of crucial system events that may require immediate action:

- **OPCOM / NOOPCOM**

- **SHUTDOWN / NOSHUTDOWN**

- **URGENT / NOURGENT**

Finally, all messages may be refused or accepted with a single command and specifying either NONE or ALL, as shown in these two examples:

```
$ SET BROADCAST=(NONE)

$ SET BROADCAST=(ALL)
```

SET TERMINAL

When you first connect to a VAX host system, the VAX establishes certain default characteristics for your terminal device. There are dozens of different characteristics for your terminal, many of which you are unlikely to alter. Later chapters discuss a few cases in which you may wish to alter the terminal characteristics. At this point we will consider some basic examples and how these characteristics are changed.

The simplest terminal characteristic is the column width of the display. Typically, the default width is 80 characters, but the SET TERMINAL command may be used to increase the width to as many as 511 characters, although most display terminals will work only up to 132 characters. The following command increases the terminal width.

```
$ SET TERMINAL/WIDTH=132
```

Another example pertains to the type of terminal device that the VAX host assigns to your terminal. While you may be using a DEC VT300 series terminal, the VAX host may not be able to recognize the device and consider the device type to be unknown. This will prohibit you from using various on-line utilities such as the editors.

The following command alters the device type setting on the VAX host for your terminal device.

```
$ SET TERMINAL/DEVICE_TYPE=VT300
```

SHOW

The SHOW command serves two basic purposes within DCL. First, it displays certain system status information, such as the system time, as we will shortly consider. Also, it parallels most of the SET options, where the user may SHOW many of the same items that were SET with the SET command.

SHOW TIME

As an example of the first use of SHOW, note the following example to display the current system date and time.

```
$ SHOW TIME
  28-JUL-1989 12:42:02
```

SHOW USERS

We may display a listing of the total number of interactive users currently logged on to our system with the SHOW USERS command. The following example displays two interactive processes, listing the user name specified during login, the default process name and the automatically generated process identification (PID) number, along with the terminal number.

```
          VAX/VMS Interactive Users
          28-JUL-1989 12:17:15.44
    Total number of interactive users = 2
  Username     Process Name      PID     Terminal
  SMITH        SMITH           00000053  VTA20:        TTA2:
  JONES        JONES           00000022  VTA19:        TTA1:
```

Users who have altered their default process name in order to provide a more descriptive name will have the result appear in the output of this command. Note the new process name for SMITH, using the name assigned from our prior example for SET PROCESS/NAME.

```
$ SHOW USERS
            VAX/VMS Interactive Users
            27-AUG-1989 14:56:43.41
   Total number of interactive users = 1

   Username      Process Name      PID    Terminal
   SMITH         J Smith x5522   0000002C  VTA1:            TTA2:
```

SHOW SYSTEM

The SHOW USERS command lists only the interactive processes created by users who have logged in. In addition, there are numerous system process and perhaps user batch processes that are active on the system at the same time. The SHOW SYSTEM command lists all processes, including the interactive processes from the SHOW USERS display, but also including system, batch and other processes. Usage and resource statistics are also displayed for each process shown. Note the sample display.

```
$ SHOW SYSTEM

VAX/VMS V5.0  on node APVAX1 28-JUL-1989 12:17:16.15    Uptime    0 03:0
   Pid      Process Name    State  Pri    I/O      CPU        Page flts
00000021 SWAPPER           HIB     16      0    0 00:00:00.41         0
00000062 JONES             LEF      4    153    0 00:00:03.54       686
00000024 JOB_CONTROL       HIB      8    149    0 00:00:01.09       115
00000025 OPCOM             LEF      8     35    0 00:00:00.60       272
00000026 NETACP            HIB      9     37    0 00:00:00.95       267
00000027 EVL               HIB      6     43    0 00:00:01.10       382
00000028 REMACP            HIB      9     23    0 00:00:00.22        75
00000053 SMITH             HIB      7    613    0 00:00:08.73      1495
```

SHOW QUOTA

In the following chapter, we will consider several file maintenance commands which allow users to create and manipulate data files. All data files use storage units called disk blocks, which are 512 bytes or characters each.

The system manager may decide to limit the number of disk blocks that a single user may consume on a disk device by enabling disk block quotas for the device. If disk quotas have been enabled, general users are not permitted to alter this quota, although you may show the disk block limit currently imposed by your quota, as well as the number of blocks currently charged against your quota.

The following command displays the current disk block quota for the user on the disk device named $DISK1:, and also the number of blocks charged against the quota, the number of blocks remaining for the quota and the permitted overdraft. (The overdraft is a number of additional disk blocks that may be temporarily available for system programs and utilities.)

```
$ SHOW QUOTA
  User [GUEST,SMITH] has 123 blocks used, 9877 available,
  of 10000 authorized and permitted overdraft of 100 blocks on $DISK1
```

SHOW PROCESS

In addition to the system and user status information we have considered, we may also use the show command to display those process characteristics that we have set with the SET command.

Our first example lists the output from the SHOW PROCESS command, which also shows the newly assigned process name.

```
$ SHOW PROCESS

27-AUG-1989 21:39:32.88   VTA1:              User: SMITH
Pid: 00000029   Proc. name: SMITH X5522     UIC: [GUEST,SMITH]
Priority:    4   Default file spec: $DISK1:[SMITH]

Devices allocated: VTA1:
$
```

SHOW BROADCAST

The parallel to the SET BROADCAST command is the SHOW BROADCAST command, which lists the current messages that are not accepted by the user terminal.

```
$ SET BROADCAST=(NOMAIL, NOPHONE, NODCL)
$ SHOW BROADCAST
Broadcasts are currently disabled for:
    PHONE
    MAIL
    DCL
$
```

SHOW TERMINAL

Finally, a complete display of all the terminal characteristics is available, including the current setting of any characteristics altered by the user with the SET TERMINAL command.

```
$ SHOW TERMINAL
Terminal: _VTA3:      Device_Type: VT200_Series  Owner: SMITH
Physical terminal: _TTA2:

    Input:   9600    LFfill: 0    Width:  80      Parity: None
    Output:  9600    CRfill: 0    Page:   24

Terminal Characteristics:
    Interactive       Echo           Type_ahead        No Escape
    No Hostsync       TTsync         Lowercase         Tab
    Wrap              Scope          No Remote         Eightbit
    Broadcast         No Readsync    No Form           Fulldup
    No Modem          No Local_echo  Autobaud          No Hangup
    No Brdcstmbx      No DMA         No Altypeahd      Set_speed
    Line Editing      Insert editing No Fallback       No Dialup
    No Secure server  Disconnect     No Pasthru        No Syspassword
    SIXEL Graphics    Soft Characters Printer port     Numeric Keypad
    ANSI_CRT          Regis          No Block_mode     Advanced_video
    Edit_mode         DEC_CRT        DEC_CRT2          No DEC_CRT3
$
```

RECALL

As you work with DCL you will often want to reexecute a command that you have recently entered. Or perhaps even more likely, you will want to recall a recent command that was incorrectly entered and make the appropriate changes. The RECALL command allows you to do these functions without retyping the command sentence.

A special buffer or storage area is automatically created when you login that saves the 20 most recent DCL commands that you have entered. You can view these commands, recall and reexecute any one of the commands, or recall, modify or correct a portion of the command sentence, and then execute the command.

When your process is deleted (that is, you log off the system) your command buffer is deleted as well. You cannot recall commands from a previous DCL session.

The following command allows you to view the command buffer of the 20 most recent commands from the current DCL session.

```
$ RECALL/ALL

 1 SHOW SYSTEM
 2 SHOW USERS
 3 SHOW QUOTA

        .
        .
        .

19 SHOW TIME
20 SET PROMPT="New prompt> "
```

If you wish to recall and reexecute the first command within the list, you may simply enter the following and press the RETURN key.

```
$ RECALL 1
$ SHOW SYSTEM
```

There are two other methods of recalling a command line. First, you may simply press the UP ARROW key. This will recall the most recent command. By pressing the UP ARROW key again, you will recall the command prior to that, and so on. Pressing the DOWN ARROW key will move you through the command buffer in the opposite direction.

Finally, you may recall a command by entering the beginning of a previous command sentence. The most recent command that begins with the characters you entered will be recalled.

```
$ RECALL SET
$ SET PROMPT="New prompt> "
```

If you wish to correct or otherwise alter a command that you have recalled before you execute it, there are a number of command editing features that are available. The table that follows lists these features. Once the command sentence has been altered, you may then press the RETURN key at any point within the command sentence and it will be executed as displayed. The newly editing command now becomes your most recent command entered and will be placed at the top of the command buffer.

Command Line Editing Keys

Key	Action
Up / Down Arrow	Recall previous / next command within buffer
Left / Right Arrow	Move cursor within command line
Delete Key	Delete previous character in command line
Control J	Delete previous word in command line
Control U	Delete to beginning of command line
Backspace Key	Move to the beginning of the line
Control E	Move to the end of the line
F14	Toggle insert / overstrike mode
Control A	Toggle insert / overstrike mode
Control R	Refresh current command line

You can clear your command buffer at any time by entering the following command. This causes the command buffer to be in a state similar to that found when you first log in.

```
$ RECALL/ERASE
```

The default editing mode for recalled commands is overstrike, although you may toggle this for any given command as described. The following option of the SET TERMINAL command will set your default editing mode to insert, requiring you to use the toggle keys in order to work in overstrike mode.

```
$ SET TERMINAL/INSERT
```

DCL Command Procedures

As we begin to consider various DCL commands and utilities, the concept of command procedures is one that is very important and useful. While command procedures can be quite complex, we will consider briefly their creation and use.

Any command that may be entered by the user interactively may be included within a text file called a command procedure. A command procedure is a series of DCL commands that the user wishes to execute sequentially. By creating a text file with a series of commands, the command procedure may be executed rather than individually entering each command within the sequence.

For instance, suppose that we wanted to regularly customize the DCL environment by using a number of the options for the SET command. Thereafter, we wanted to use the parallel options of the SHOW command, among other options, to list status information. Rather than repeatedly entering these commands day after day, we may use the CREATE command (considered in more detail in the next chapter) to create a file named SET_UP.COM, that contains the following commands:

```
$ CREATE SET_UP.COM

$ SET PROMPT="New prompt> "
$ SET PROCESS/NAME="SMITH x5522"
$ SET CONTROL=(T,Y)
$ SHOW PROCESS
$ SHOW TIME
$ SHOW USERS
^ Z
```

Having created the command procedure, whenever we wish to execute the series of commands listed within the procedure, we need only execute the procedure. Command procedures are executed by using the @ command and naming the command procedure, as follows:

```
$ @ SET_UP.COM
```

All of the options of the SET command that we have considered, with the exception of SET PASSWORD, affect only the current user process and session. If we want the same options for another session, we must enter the commands again in the new session. While we could include the commands within a command procedure, as just shown, we must still remember to execute the procedure for every new session.

A helpful option is the use of a command procedure known as LOGIN.COM. Whenever a user logs in and an interactive process is created, the command procedure LOGIN.COM is retrieved from the default directory and automatically executed. Thus, by creating a procedure with the name LOGIN.COM and including within it commands that are effective only for a single session, the user may recreate the desired environment each time he or she logs in to begin a new interactive session.

During the exercises for this chapter we will demonstrate a sample use of the LOGIN.COM command procedure.

Chapter Two Exercises

Perform the following exercises, referring back to the examples within this chapter for the precise syntax, rules and expected output.

Exercise 1

a) Change the default DCL prompt with the SET PROMPT command.

b) Using the same command, change back to the default prompt.

c) Using the SET PROCESS/NAME command, specify a new process name.

d) Use the SHOW PROCESS, SHOW USERS and SHOW SYSTEM commands to note the changed process name.

e) Using the SET PASSWORD command, alter your password. Be sure to remember the changed password so that you can log in again. Logout and login again, using the new password you have defined.

f) Use the SET CONTROL command to activate the CONTROL T and Y functions. While executing a command or utility, such as HELP or SHOW SYSTEM, press CONTROL T several times and note the display.

g) While executing HELP or SHOW SYSTEM, press CONTROL Y to interrupt the process. Thereafter, enter CONTINUE as the next command to continue processing without any detrimental effect.

h) Screen out certain system and utility messages with the SET BROADCAST command.

i) Alter the terminal width to 132 characters with the SET TERMINAL command and enter any SHOW command to note the new display width. Reset the terminal width back to 80 characters.

Exercise 2

Using the SHOW command, attempt the following options on your system and examine the output:

a) SHOW TIME

b) SHOW USERS and identify your own interactive process among the list of other interactive processes.

c) SHOW SYSTEM and identify your own interactive process among the list of all system processes.

d) SHOW QUOTA

e) SHOW BROADCAST

f) SHOW TERMINAL

Exercise 3

As you begin to use DCL and learn its format and rules, you will likely make several syntax errors entering the commands. Initially, it will probably be quicker and easier for you to simply reenter the entire command. However, it would be to your advantage to force yourself to use the RECALL command to recall the incorrect command, modify it, and reexecute it. As you first use the RECALL command, this will likely take you more time than simply reentering the command from scratch. In the long run, though, becoming familiar with the RECALL command and its various options will save a significant amount of time within DCL.

In order to become familiar with RECALL, attempt the following:

a) Use RECALL/ALL to list the last 20 commands within this session.

b) Using the following recall methods, explained earlier, recall and reexecute a command:

- Recall by number
- Recall by command name
- Recall by pressing the up and down arrows until the command is located

c) Recall a command with one of the available methods and modify the command. Use the command line editing keys listed in the table within this chapter to modify the command line. Reexecute the modified command.

d) Erase the command buffer with RECALL/ERASE and then examine the blank buffer with RECALL/ALL.

e) Enter the command SET TERMINAL/INSERT to change the default to insert mode for command editing. Recall and modify a command and note the insert mode that is now in use.

Exercise 4

Having considered several DCL commands, we will now illustrate the use of a simple command procedure, in particular, the LOGIN.COM file.

Let us assume that each time we logged in, we wished to customize our environment by creating a unique DCL prompt and a user-assigned process name. Of course, we could enter the SET PROMPT and SET PROCESS/NAME commands at the start of each session, or we could create a text file named LOGIN.COM and include these commands within the file. Thus, each time we log in, the commands within the LOGIN.COM file will automatically be executed, before we even receive the DCL dollar sign prompt.

In subsequent chapters, we will consider several different methods of creating text files, to be used as command procedures, as memo documents or for other purposes. For the present, let us simply say that the following command will allow us to create a simple LOGIN.COM procedure.

```
$ CREATE LOGIN.COM
```

Once we have entered the above command and pressed the RETURN key, the cursor will be positioned on the next line, awaiting text to be entered within the file. Enter the following text exactly as shown, including the dollar sign, and press RETURN. Be sure to enter the text carefully.

```
$ SET PROMPT="New prompt> "
```

Note

You may use the DELETE key on your keyboard to backup
and retype any characters within the line that are incorrect.
However, once you press the RETURN key and go on to the
next line, you cannot go back and correct the line. If you make
a mistake in typing that you cannot correct, press the
CONTROL Y key. This will bring you back to the DCL
prompt and you may create the file again with the CREATE
LOGIN.COM command.

Enter the next line of text as follows, again including the dollar sign at the
beginning of the line, and press CONTROL Z.

```
$ SET PROCESS/NAME="Our process"
```

We have now created a command procedure named LOGIN.COM which includes
the two commands that we have entered. Like any command procedure, we may
execute the command immediately by entering the following command. The
commands will be read by DCL from the LOGIN.COM file and executed exactly
the same as if we entered them ourselves.

```
$ @ LOGIN.COM
```

You will notice that the DCL prompt has been changed as we have requested.
Enter the SHOW USERS command and you will notice that the process name
has also been changed.

Each time that you log in, the commands within the LOGIN.COM file will
automatically execute. Logoff and login again, and notice that the DCL prompt
and the process name have been automatically set according to your
specifications.

Recreate another LOGIN.COM file by adding several additional commands.
Execute the procedure either with the @ or by logging off and back on again and
watch the results of the procedure.

Exercise Answers

Many exercises are self-explanatory and need no answers. Where applicable, the answers to exercises are stated herein.

The caret (^) character is used to indicate the pressing of a control key. Thus ^Y indicates the user pressing of CONTROL Y, ^Z indicates CONTROL Z, and so on.

Exercise 1a

```
$ SET PROMPT="New prompt> "
```

Exercise 1b

```
$ SET PROMPT
```

Exercise 1c

```
$ SET PROCESS/NAME="My name"
```

Exercise 1d

```
$ SHOW PROCESS
$ SHOW USERS
$ SHOW SYSTEM
```

Exercise 1e

```
$ SET PASSWORD
```

Exercise 1f

```
$ SET CONTROL=(T,Y)
```

Exercise 1g

```
$  HELP
^  Y
$  CONTINUE
```

Exercise 1h

```
$  SET  BROADCAST=(NOPHONE,NOMAIL,NODCL)
```

Exercise 1i

```
$  SET  TERMINAL/WIDTH=132
$  SHOW  SYSTEM
$  SET  TERMINAL/WIDTH=80
```

Exercise 2a-2f

Self-explanatory

Exercise 3a-3e

Self-explanatory

Exercise 4, first LOGIN.COM file with commands indicated within the exercise.

```
$  CREATE  LOGIN.COM
$  SET  PROMPT="New  prompt>  "
$  SET  PROCESS/NAME="Our  process"
^  Z
$  @LOGIN.COM
```

Exercise 4, recreated LOGIN.COM file with commands of the user's choice. The following is a possible example of commands that may be used.

```
$  CREATE  LOGIN.COM
$  SHOW  USERS
$  SHOW  SYSTEM
$  SHOW  TIME
^  Z
$  @LOGIN.COM
```

Chapter Three

File Maintenance Commands

Overview

The purpose of this chapter is to describe the DCL commands available for working with and maintaining data files on the VAX. As the previous chapter stated, all VAX data is stored within disk files. These files may include the sample memo files used in our examples that are created by users within an editor. Other files include command procedures, programs and large data base files.

As we mentioned at the outset, most DCL commands are quite intuitive and, therefore, easier to remember. This is especially true of the file commands that we will now consider. The list of commands discussed within this chapter are:

- CREATE
- DIRECTORY (basic options only)
- TYPE
- COPY
- RENAME
- APPEND
- DELETE
- PURGE

CREATE

We considered some information regarding the CREATE command within the exercises of the last chapter. The CREATE command enabled us to create a command procedure file. This command allows the user to create any text file. To begin this process, simply type the command at the dollar sign prompt, followed by a file name and extension of your choice.

```
$ CREATE WEEK_ONE.MEMO
```

The rules we discussed for the VMS file specification can be illustrated here. We omitted a network system name along with a device and directory name. Therefore, VMS will assume that we wish to create the file on our local system and in our personal default device and directory.

If there happens to already exist a file by the same name within our directory, we do not erase the information that it contains. Rather, VMS will create a new version of the file, allowing us to read the original information with other DCL commands by including the version number with the file name at that time.

Once you enter the above command, you may then type in any information you wish, ending each line with the RETURN key. Once you have entered the information, you can close the file and return to the DCL prompt by pressing the CONTROL Z (^Z) key.

```
$ CREATE WEEK_ONE.MEMO
Dear Mr. Smith:

The project status for week one is as follows...
   .
   .
   .
^ Z
```

The disadvantage to creating files in this manner is the lack of editing features. Once you have typed in a line and pressed the RETURN key to go to the next line, you cannot go back and modify any previous lines that may contain mistakes. (You can, however, use the DELETE key to correct previous characters within the current line that you are on.)

For this reason, use the CREATE command to quickly and simply create small files. Most files, however, should be created with one of the VMS editors, such as EVE or EDT (discussed later), that allow you to modify any portion of a file or document, and also provide other powerful editing features.

Whenever a file is created, using either the CREATE command, one of the editors or some other method, the following file functions occur:

- The date and time the file was created is recorded for the file.

- The creator of the file is recorded and will subsequently be considered the owner of the file. (The owner assigned to a file relates to file security, which is considered in Chapter 6, "File Protection and Control").

- The file is assigned disk blocks from the storage device to store the data contained within the file. Extra disk blocks may also be assigned, although currently unused, for expansion of the file at a later time.

- Each file also has a modification date in addition to the creation date. When a file is initially created and assigned version number one, the modification date and the creation date are the same. While it may differ depending upon the modification method used, generally, whenever the file is later modified and a new file version is created, a new modification date is assigned to the new file version, while the creation date remains the same.

DIRECTORY

This command displays a list of the files stored within your personal directory or if requested, within another user's directory. Only a brief discussion of this command is considered here. Within chapter 4, "Directories," we will consider more detailed information regarding directories, subdirectories and the DIRECTORY command.

The following example displays the files stored within your personal default directory.

```
$ DIRECTORY

Directory $DISK1:[SMITH]

FILE1.MEMO;2        FILE1.MEMO;1        FILE2.MEMO;1        FILE3.MEMO;1
LOGIN.COM;8         OUT.LIS;1

Total of 6 files.
$
```

You will notice there are duplicate copies of some files, but with different version numbers. This indicates files that have been modified, with the older versions automatically retained. The DIRECTORY command also totals the number of files currently stored within the directory.

Subject to security restrictions, you may be able to view the list of files contained within another user's directory by adding a directory specification to the command line. The next example lists the files within the directory of [JONES], which is located on the same system and the same device as [SMITH].

```
Directory $DISK1:[JONES]

LOGIN.COM;8          PHONE_LIST.DAT;1

Total of 2 files.
$
```

We may list files within directories that are stored on other disk devices or other systems by simply being more specific within the directory specification and explicitly stating the system name and the device name, rather than just using the assumed default values. The first example would list the files within the directory of [SMITH] that are stored on another device, DUA5:. The second example would list files stored on another system by explicitly naming the full directory.

```
$ DIRECTORY DUA5:[SMITH]

$ DIRECTORY LONDON::DUA2:[JONES]
```

TYPE

This command allows users to display on the terminal screen, or TYPE out to the terminal, the contents of a text file. For example, if we wanted to type out the contents of the weekly status memo file created earlier with the CREATE command, we could enter the following:

```
$ TYPE WEEK_ONE.MEMO
Dear Mr. Smith:

The project status for week one is as follows...
  .
  .
  .
$
```

We may include several files within the type operation by adding the file names to the end of the command, separated by commas. This feature, known as a parameter list and discussed in more detail later within this chapter, is available for most of the other file maintenance commands as well.

```
$ TYPE WEEK_ONE.MEMO, WEEK_TWO.MEMO,
WEEK_THREE.MEMO
```

We can use the TYPE command to illustrate the rules and concepts discussed for the VMS file specification. If we had, for instance, several versions of the file WEEK_ONE.MEMO, the above command would have selected the most recent version by default due to the fact that we had not named any specific version number. However, if we wanted to display the original version of the file, we could simply specify the version number we want, rather than just taking the implied default:

```
$ TYPE WEEK_ONE.MEMO;1
```

If the file was contained on another disk drive and in another individual's directory, such as [JONES], rather than our own, we could still type out the contents of the file by being more specific in the file specification and overriding the implied defaults. (Once again, however, we must have been granted permission to read files that we do not own).

```
$ TYPE DUA5:[JONES]WEEK_ONE.MEMO
```

We can also illustrate wildcards once again. Suppose that we wanted to type out all the versions of all the .MEMO files within JONES' account. We could enter the following:

```
$ TYPE DUA5:[JONES]*.MEMO;*
```

If the file that is being typed out contains more data than can be displayed on the terminal screen, the display of the file will "scroll up" as quickly as the data can be displayed. This means that the user will not be able to see the data on the initial pages of the file. To prevent this occurrence, users may select the /PAGE option for the TYPE command. With this option, only one page of data from the file is displayed before the display temporarily halts. The user is prompted to press the RETURN key in order to display the next page from the file, and so on, until the entire file is typed out.

When being prompted for a RETURN, the user may also press CONTROL Z (the EXIT function) to exit from the type function and return to DCL command level.

Note the sample output from the TYPE/PAGE WEEK_TWO.MEMO command:

```
Dear Mr. Smith:

Please be advised of the status regarding the second week of our projec

The status of the project is as follows...

  .

  .

                    Press RETURN to continue
```

COPY

This command creates a file using the data from an existing file, that is, copying the data from an existing input file to a new output file. In addition to the copy command itself, the user must specify the name of the file to copy from (the input file specification), and the name of the file to copy to (the output file specification).

Our first example creates the file WEEK_TWO.MEMO using the data from the input file WEEK_ONE.MEMO.

```
$ COPY WEEK_ONE.MEMO WEEK_TWO.MEMO
```

If the file WEEK_TWO.MEMO already exists, a new version of WEEK_TWO.MEMO is created. In any case, the input file is never modified.

If we wanted to copy a file from SMITH's directory to JONES' directory, we could do so simply by being more specific within the file specifications, as shown below.

```
$ COPY [SMITH]WEEK_ONE.MEMO [JONES]STATUS.MEMO
```

As shown in the next example, the new copy of the file may receive the same file name and extension as the original or input file by using the asterisk in place of a new file name. This states that the output file should use the identical file name as the input file.

```
$ COPY [SMITH]WEEK_ONE.MEMO [JONES]*
```

The basic concepts for wildcards that we have already considered several times will naturally apply here with the COPY command. For instance, if we wanted to copy all memo files from SMITH's directory to JONES' directory, retaining the original file names, we would enter the following:

```
$ COPY [SMITH]*.MEMO [JONES]*
```

If a file was inadvertently or improperly modified, the most recent version of the file may contain invalid data. However, due to the retention of older versions by VMS, a previous version of the file hopefully contains the correct data. We can use the COPY command to make an older version the most recent and, therefore, the default, version of the file.

To illustrate, suppose that the file WEEK_ONE.MEMO had been incorrectly modified, rendering the more recent versions useless. By using the TYPE command and looking at all the versions of the file, we determine that version 2 is the most recent version that contains valid data. We would like to restore the file so that version 2 is the latest. Using the COPY command, we may enter the following:

```
$ COPY WEEK_ONE.MEMO;2 WEEK_ONE.MEMO
```

The command states that the input file is version 2 of the memo file. The output file uses the same file name, without any version number. As COPY begins to create the output file, it detects that there are prior versions and therefore creates a new version of the file. The net effect is that a new, latest version of WEEK_ONE.MEMO is created using the data from the last valid version of the file, version 2. Thus, we have, in effect, "rolled back" the file to version 2.

RENAME

This command changes the name of a file from its original name to a new name. Unlike the COPY command which creates a duplicate copy of the information under a new name, the RENAME command simply changes the name of the file. It no longer exists under its old name. No changes are made to the data within the file.

In addition to the RENAME command itself, we must identify the current name of the file and the new name to be assigned. Suppose that we wanted to change the file name WEEK_ONE.MEMO to a more concise WEEK1.MEMO, without, of course, altering any of the data contained within. This would be accomplished as follows:

```
$ RENAME WEEK_ONE.MEMO WEEK1.MEMO
```

Wildcards are, of course, available for use with the file specifications of the RENAME command, as we have considered. The following command changes the file name extension of all .MEMO files to a more abbreviated .MEM.

```
$ RENAME *.MEMO *.MEM
```

In the above examples, we did not specify a device and directory name. Hence, we have been working with files contained within our default personal directory. Subject to the standard security features of VMS, we may use the RENAME command to rename the location portions of the VMS file specification, rather than the file name itself. In this case, we are actually performing a "move" more than a rename, although we are still renaming at least a portion of the file specification.

To illustrate, if we wanted to move the file WEEK1.MEMO contained within the directory [SMITH] to the directory [JONES], we could use the following RENAME command and rename the directory portion of the file specification. By using the asterisk on the output file specification, we retain the original name. The end result is that the file WEEK1.MEMO is moved from the directory [SMITH] to the directory [JONES] while retaining the same file name.

```
$ RENAME [SMITH]WEEK1.MEMO [JONES]*
```

Note

Moving a file in this manner by using the RENAME command is only permitted if the new location has the same system name and device name as the old location. To move a file to another system or device, use the COPY command.

APPEND

The append command appends the contents of one or more files to a second file. We must specify the file to be used for input and the file to which it will be appended. The first example appends the contents of the file DAY1.MEMO to the file WEEK1.MEMO

```
$ APPEND DAY1.MEMO WEEK1.MEMO
```

Several files may be appended onto another single file. For instance, perhaps we wanted to append the daily status memos that we have created for each day of the week onto a single memo file for the entire week. Multiple files may be included within the operation either by means of wildcards or a parameter list.

The following examples illustrate both methods.

```
$ APPEND DAY%.MEMO WEEK1.MEMO

$ APPEND DAY1.MEMO,DAY2.MEMO,DAY3.MEMO WEEK1.MEMO
```

If the file that we are appending to does not exist, and hence there is no place for DCL to append the data, an error message will be generated. However, we may circumvent this problem with the /NEW_VERSION qualifier, instructing DCL to create a new version of the output file.

This same qualifier may be used to create a new version of the output file when one already exists.

```
$ APPEND/NEW_VERSION DAY%.MEMO WEEK1.MEMO
```

DELETE

This command deletes a file from the storage device. Once deleted, it is no longer available. Consistent with the format of other commands already discussed, we must state the VMS file specification that identifies the file we wish to delete.

```
$ DELETE WEEK_ONE.MEMO;1
```

As the DELETE command erases data, the user obviously should be certain before entering the command that the file name specified is the correct file for the delete operation. As part of the caution that should be used for this command, DCL will not assume a file version number. Hence, unlike other commands, a version number must be specified as part of the file name, as shown above.

An asterisk wildcard may be used for the version number, indicating that all versions are to be deleted. Or, the most recent version may be implied by entering a semicolon and no version number. But in all cases, the version number must be stated or implied by means of the semicolon. Note the following examples that illustrate these two possibilities with the DELETE command.

```
$ DELETE WEEK_ONE.MEMO;*
```

```
$ DELETE WEEK_ONE.MEMO;
```

Parameter lists are permitted in order to delete several files with a single command.

```
$ DELETE DAY1.MEMO;*, DAY2.MEMO;*, DAY3.MEMO;*
```

Whenever a file is deleted, the space used by the file on the disk is marked by the system as available space and will eventually be used by a new file that is created on that disk. However, until the space is reused, the data from the deleted file is still actually on the disk and potentially available to an unauthorized user. The /ERASE option eliminates this risk as it writes a pattern of data over the space used by the deleted file at the time of deletion. Therefore, the data is immediately destroyed.

```
$ DELETE/ERASE DAY%.MEMO;*
```

PURGE

As you are now well aware, new versions of files are generally created when a file is modified. This provides the DCL user with insurance against inadvertent modification of files, allowing a file to be rolled back to an earlier version, as we described with the COPY command.

When files have not been inadvertently modified, but properly modified, the retention of all older versions can become bothersome and very consumptive of disk space. Remember that the disk blocks used by files within our directory, which includes all the various versions of specific files, are charged against our overall disk quota. Especially if files are modified frequently, a large amount of storage space may be unnecessarily wasted on the older versions.

The PURGE command deletes the older versions of all files specified, retaining only the most recent version. By default, all files within our default directory are purged.

Notice in the following example the older versions of the files FILE1.MEMO and WEEK_ONE.MEMO. After the PURGE command, only the most recent version of these files exists.

```
Directory $DISK1:[SMITH]

FILE1.MEMO;2        FILE1.MEMO;1        FILE2.MEMO;1        FILE3.MEMO;1
LOGIN.COM;8         WEEK_ONE.MEMO;5     WEEK_ONE.MEMO;4     WEEK_ONE.MEMO;3
WEEK_ONE.MEMO;2     WEEK_ONE.MEMO;1     WEEK_TWO.MEMO;2     WEEK_TWO.MEMO;1

Total of 12 files.
$ PURGE
$ DIRECTORY

Directory $DISK1:[SMITH]

FILE1.MEMO;2        FILE2.MEMO;1        FILE3.MEMO;1        LOGIN.COM;8
WEEK_ONE.MEMO;5     WEEK_TWO.MEMO;2

Total of 6 files.
$
```

Alternately, we may specify a single file to be purged. Or, by using wildcards and parameter lists, we may purge a number of files with a single command. All these possible functions are illustrated below.

```
$ PURGE DAY1.MEMO

$ PURGE DAY1.MEMO, DAY2.MEMO, DAY3.MEMO

$ PURGE DAY%.MEMO
```

Files from another directory may be purged, provided that we have the privilege to delete files in the directory specified.

```
$ PURGE [SMITH]

$ PURGE [JONES]
```

We may qualify the purge function, instructing DCL to retain more than just the most recent version of files, but rather to keep several additional versions. The following command retains the three most recent versions of the files specified.

```
$ PURGE/KEEP=3 DAY%.MEMO
```

Command Qualifiers

You have no doubt noticed that there are several options available for each command that qualifies the specific manner in which the command is executed. These options are known as qualifiers.

As an example, consider the first command that we discussed, the LOGOUT command. Recall that we had the option during the logout process of having VMS display certain statistics regarding our session on the VAX. This was done by entering the LOGOUT command with the /FULL qualifier, as follows:

```
$ LOGOUT/FULL
```

As you may have observed, the qualifiers are attached to the command itself, but separated by a slash (/).

As another example, we considered the /PAGE qualifier for the TYPE command. This altered or qualified the manner in which we wanted the TYPE command to operate, by displaying only a single page of data at a time.

```
$ TYPE/PAGE *.MEMO
```

In harmony with the logical structure of the DCL language, there are numerous qualifiers that are common to several different commands. Particularly is this true with the file maintenance commands that we have discussed within this chapter.

/LOG

We will first consider the /LOG qualifier. This qualifier causes the command that we have entered to generate a log message on the terminal screen informing the user that the command has successfully occurred. This is especially useful for commands that do not normally generate any output. Notice, in the example below, the difference in the COPY command when the /LOG qualifier is used.

```
$ COPY WEEK_ONE.MEMO NEW.MEMO
$
$ COPY/LOG WEEK_ONE.MEMO NEW.MEMO
%COPY-S-COPIED, $DISK1:[SMITH]WEEK_ONE.MEMO;5 copied to $DISK1:[SMITH]NEW.MEMO
(1 block)
$
```

This same qualifier is applicable for several other commands. If, for example, we wanted a similar log message for an APPEND command, we would simply enter the following.

```
$ APPEND/LOG DAY1.MEMO WEEK1.MEMO
```

The following commands that we have considered permit the use of the /LOG qualifier:

- APPEND
- COPY
- CREATE
- DELETE
- PURGE
- RENAME

/CONFIRM

The /CONFIRM qualifier states that the command being used will request a confirmation entry by the user before actually performing the command. This is especially useful when the multiple files have been specified with wildcards.

To illustrate, suppose that we wished to delete certain files. We could specify with wildcards a number of different files. With the /CONFIRM qualifier, before each file specified is actually deleted, the user is asked to confirm whether or not the file should in fact be deleted. Note the following example:

```
$ DELETE/CONFIRM *.MEMO;*
$DISK1:[SMITH]FILE1.MEMO;2, delete? [N]:
$DISK1:[SMITH]FILE2.MEMO;1, delete? [N]:
$DISK1:[SMITH]FILE3.MEMO;1, delete? [N]:
$DISK1:[SMITH]NEW.MEMO;2, delete? [N]:
$DISK1:[SMITH]NEW.MEMO;1, delete? [N]:Y
$DISK1:[SMITH]WEEK_ONE.MEMO;5, delete? [N]:
$DISK1:[SMITH]WEEK_TWO.MEMO;2, delete? [N]:
$
```

As we can see, before the delete operation is performed on any file, the user is asked to confirm the delete. By entering entering N (or pressing RETURN to accept the default answer of N) the user does not confirm the file for deletion and the file is not deleted. By entering Y, the user confirms the delete for that file and the command proceeds on to the next file.

When the user is prompted for a confirmation, the following entries, or abbreviations of these entries, are accepted as valid responses to confirm the operation:

- YES
- TRUE
- 1

The following entries, or abbreviations of these entries, are accepted as valid responses to refuse, or not confirm, the operation:

- NO
- FALSE
- 0

Lastly, the following entries are also accepted and result in the actions described:

- ALL confirms for the current file and any others included within this function. No additional confirmation requests are made for this command.

- QUIT refuses or does not confirm the current file and any others included within this function. No additional confirmation requests are made for this command.

- CONTROL Z indicates the EXIT function and is identical to QUIT.

The following commands considered within this chapter permit the use of the /CONFIRM qualifier to request user confirmation of all files considered:

- APPEND
- COPY
- CREATE
- DELETE
- PURGE
- RENAME
- TYPE

/BEFORE
/SINCE

We stated during our consideration of the CREATE command that whenever a command is initially created, whether with the CREATE command, an editor or some other function, various file attributes are also noted, such as the creation date and the modification date for the file. (There is also an expiration date and a backup date recorded for the file, although these are not considered within this textbook.)

Thus far, when we have specified files for file maintenance commands, we have stated either a specific file or files, or used wildcards to indicate various files. We may also use the /BEFORE and /SINCE qualifiers along with the /CREATED qualifier to select only those files that have been created before or since the date indicated.

In the following example, we specify that all files with an extension of .MEMO should be included in the TYPE operation. However, with the addition of the /CREATE/SINCE qualifiers, we further specify that only those .MEMO files that have been created since the date indicated should be included. (Note carefully the required format for specifying a date within VMS).

```
$ TYPE/CREATED/SINCE=15-FEB-1989 *.MEMO
```

Similarly, we could have selected files created before a certain date as follows:

```
$ TYPE/CREATED/BEFORE=15-FEB-1989 *.MEMO
```

We could be even more specific by identifying files according to their time of creation. The time is specified according to a 24-hour or international time format. The next example selects only those .MEMO files created before one o'clock in the afternoon of the 15th of February in the year 1989. (Again, carefully note the required format for both the date and time, including the colons).

```
$ TYPE/CREATED/BEFORE=15-FEB-1989:13:00 *.MEMO
```

There are several keywords available from DCL that represent yesterday's date, today's and tomorrow's. Rather than entering these dates according to the VMS date format, we could alternately use these keywords.

- YESTERDAY
- TODAY
- TOMORROW

Note the example below:

```
$ TYPE/CREATED/SINCE=TODAY *.MEMO

$ TYPE/CREATED/BEFORE=YESTERDAY *.MEMO
```

Likewise, we may select files according to the modification date. When specifying the modification date, we may also include a specific time of day or use the keywords for yesterday, today and tomorrow.

```
$ TYPE/MODIFIED/SINCE=15-FEB-1989:13:00 *.MEMO

$ TYPE/MODIFIED/SINCE=TODAY *.MEMO
```

Although we will not consider the use of the expiration and backup dates for files within this textbook, let us simply state at this point that we may select files based upon these dates, as shown below:

```
$ TYPE/BACKUP/SINCE=15-FEB-1989:13:00 *.MEMO

$ TYPE/EXPIRED/BEFORE=YESTERDAY *.MEMO
```

The following summarizes the qualifiers to select files before or since the dates indicated. The /CREATE qualifier is the assumed default when using /BEFORE or /SINCE and is therefore optional:

- /CREATED
- /MODIFIED
- /BACKUP
- /EXPIRED

The following commands that we have considered permit the use of the /BEFORE and /SINCE qualifiers:

- APPEND
- COPY
- CREATE
- DELETE
- DIRECTORY
- PURGE
- RENAME
- TYPE

/EXCLUDE

The /EXCLUDE qualifier permits the specific exclusion of certain files that would otherwise have been selected for the command due to the file names, wildcards or /BEFORE and /SINCE qualifiers.

In the following example with the TYPE command, we use the asterisk wildcard to select all .MEMO files and we use the /BEFORE qualifier to indicate files created before a certain date. However, we will supplement these indications with the /EXCLUDE qualifier to specifically exclude out of the operation the files IMPORTANT.MEMO and URGENT.MEMO.

```
$ TYPE                           -
/CREATED                         -
/BEFORE=15-FEB-1989              -
/EXCLUDE=(IMPORTANT.MEMO,URGENT.MEMO)  *.MEMO
```

Note

The dash (-) character at the end of each line within the above command is known as the command continuation character. Whenever a command sentence becomes so lengthy that it is not easily legible, the user may enter only a portion of the command line and enter the dash character followed by a RETURN. This allows subsequent portions of the same command sentence to be entered on several different lines. This is not required, however, as the command line will automatically wrap around to the next terminal line. For the sake of simplicity, it is suggested that the reader enter these sample commands on his or her system without the command continuation character and simply allow the command sentence to wrap around. Be sure, though, to enter the space that separates the qualifiers from the file name parameter.

The following file maintenance commands permit the use of the /EXCLUDE qualifier:

- APPEND
- COPY
- CREATE
- DELETE
- DIRECTORY
- PURGE
- RENAME
- TYPE

/OUTPUT

Those commands that normally generate a display of information to the terminal screen may collect the displayed information and alternately store it within an output file.

As an example, suppose that we wanted to generate a directory listing of the files within our directory with the DIRECTORY command. However, rather than having the display appear on our terminal screen, we would like the output to be saved to a text file. Thereafter, we may access the text file and print it on a printer, or mail the output to another user, or perhaps modify the output with one of the editors. While we will consider these functions within later chapters, the /OUTPUT qualifier discussed here does create the output text file that we will later use.

The following DIRECTORY command generates no output on the terminal screen. However, by typing out the output file used by the DIRECTORY command, we can see that we have successfully collected the output into a text file.

```
$ DIRECTORY/OUTPUT=DIR_OUTPUT.FILE
$ TYPE DIR_OUTPUT.FILE

Directory $DISK1:[SMITH]

DIR_OUTPUT.FILE;1   FILE1.MEMO;2      FILE2.MEMO;1      FILE3.MEMO;1
LOGIN.COM;8         NEW.MEMO;2        WEEK_ONE.MEMO;5   WEEK_TWO.MEMO;2

Total of 8 files.
$
```

Most of the file maintenance commands considered within this chapter simply perform a function, such as COPY or DELETE, and do not generate any output listing of information. The following commands, however, do generate output and therefore permit the use of the /OUTPUT qualifier.

- DIRECTORY
- TYPE

You may recall, though, that we have already considered a number of other commands within the earlier chapters that do generate output to terminal screen, particularly the SHOW commands. The following SHOW commands that we have considered permit the use of the /OUTPUT qualifier.

- SHOW USERS
- SHOW SYSTEM
- SHOW PROCESS
- SHOW BROADCAST
- SHOW TERMINAL

Combinations of Qualifiers

Finally, we will briefly consider some examples of how several different qualifiers may be included within the same command sentence to provide a very unique and specific function based upon the specific need of a user.

In our first example, we will request a DIRECTORY listing of the files within the [JONES] directory. However, we will select files based upon the following criteria:

- Created before today.
- Excluding files that have a file name extension of either .MEMO or .COM.
- Sending the output to a text file.

The following command sentence would perform such an operation.

```
$ DIRECTORY                    -
/CREATED                       -
/BEFORE=TODAY                  -
/EXCLUDE=(*.MEMO, *.COM)       -
/OUTPUT=OUTPUT.FILE  [JONES]
```

In our next example, we will perform a delete operation based upon the following specifications:

- Select all files modified since yesterday.
- Request a confirmation from the user for each file selected.
- Generate a log message after each file has been deleted.

The following command sentence would perform this operation:

```
$ DELETE          -
/MODIFIED         -
/SINCE=YESTERDAY  -
/CONFIRM          -
/LOG  *.*;*
```

DCL Grammatical Rules

It is appropriate at this point to consider the formal rules and structure of a DCL command sentence. Examining the commands we have considered thus far, you may begin to wonder if there is any structure to the syntax shown. For example, some parts of a command must be prefaced by a slash (/), other portions must be separated by commas (,) or perhaps a space, and so on.

All these various differences can be summed up in a few simple rules. The purpose of this chapter is to present these rules and illustrate their use with commands that we have already considered. We will consider the rules for the following portions of the DCL command sentence:

- Verb
- Parameter
- Qualifier

Verb

The first part of a DCL command sentence is the command itself or the verb. The verb describes *what* is to be done, such as DELETE, TYPE, LOGOUT, etc. The rules for specifying verbs are as follows:

- The verb must be the first portion of the command sentence, immediately following the dollar sign ($) prompt.

- Verbs may be abbreviated to at least the first four characters. The characters DELE would suffice for DELETE, the characters LOGO for LOGOUT, and so on.

- Some verbs are unique among other DCL verbs with even fewer than four characters, and may thus be abbreviated further. For instance, DEL is a valid abbreviation for DELETE as no other DCL verb currently begins with the characters DEL, LO is a currently valid abbreviation for LOGOUT, etc.

Parameters

Parameters follow the verb. There are a number of exceptions, but oftentimes a parameter is a VMS file specification and specifies *where* the data exists that the verb should operate upon. For example, the TYPE verb must be followed by a parameter that is a VMS file specification. This parameter states *where* the verb will find the data to type.

The following examples illustrate command sentences with verbs that include parameters for a full VMS file specification or a portion of the specification, such as the directory.

```
$ TYPE [SMITH.MEMOS.JAN]DAY1.MEMO

$ DIRECTORY [SMITH.FILES]
```

Some commands, such as COPY, APPEND, RENAME and others, include two parameters, an input file specification and an output file specification.

```
$ COPY DAY1.MEMO OLD.MEMO
```

Note

Among the many exceptions to the above mentioned rule of parameters being used for file specifications are the SET and SHOW commands. These commands require, as the first parameter, a key word that identifies what is being set or shown, such as DEFAULT, TERMINAL, BROADCAST and others.

Some command verbs have required parameters, others have optional parameters. Using the above examples, you may recall that the DIRECTORY command verb may be used without any parameter, with DCL assuming that the directory you wish to list is the current default. However, the TYPE, COPY and other commands have required parameters. DCL does not assume which file you wish to type out if you do not specify one, nor does it assume which files you wish to copy if you do not specify them. Hence, these commands have required parameters.

If you enter a DCL verb that has required parameters, but you do not include the required parameters, DCL will prompt for them automatically. Note the following verbs entered without any parameters:

```
$  TYPE
_File:

$  COPY DAY1.MEMO
_To:

$  SET
_What:  DEFAULT
_Directory:
```

Thus, you do not really have to remember the required parameters for a verb or even the order in which multiple parameters are required. You can simply enter the verb and let DCL prompt for the parameters and in the proper order.

The syntax for parameters is quite simple. All parameters are separated from the verb by a space. If there are multiple parameters, such as the input and the output specification for the COPY command, the parameters are separated from each other with a space also.

Our final comment on parameters deals with parameter lists, something referred to in an earlier chapter. Some commands permit you to enter several instances of the same parameter. This is a parameter list. Note the following TYPE command. TYPE has only one parameter, the VMS file specification of the file you wish to type out; however, several instances of the parameter are permitted, separated by commas, thereby creating a parameter list.

```
$  TYPE DAY1.MEMO, DAY2.MEMO, DAY3.MEMO
```

The following COPY command provides another example. The command sentence includes several instances of the first parameter, while the second parameter, the output specification, indicates a retention of the original file names.

```
$  COPY DAY1.MEMO, DAY2.MEMO, DAY3.MEMO [JONES]*
```

Qualifiers

A DCL command sentence may consist solely of the verb, and perhaps one or more required or optional parameters. A qualifier, as the name implies, qualifies the action of the verb, or states *how* you wish to do what the verb will perform.

You are already familiar with a number of qualifiers, but note once again the use of qualifiers in embellishing the verb, or stating how you wish to do the command.

```
$ DIRECTORY/SIZE

$ TYPE/PAGE DAY1.MEMO
```

The rules for qualifiers are as follows:

- The qualifier should generally follow immediately after the verb, separated by a slash. (This location or placement of the qualifier is not always mandatory, although it is recommended. The slash is always required.)

- Qualifiers for one command are generally valid for other commands, where this makes logical sense. Thus, you need not necessarily memorize dozens of qualifiers for dozens of verbs. They are generally consistent for many different verbs.

- More than one qualifier may be used for the same command sentence. There are some instances, though, where two qualifiers may be mutually exclusive.

- Qualifiers may also be abbreviated to at least the first four characters, and perhaps less if they continue to be unique.

Chapter 3 Exercises

Perform the following exercises to utilize the file maintenance commands within this chapter. Refer back to the many examples within this chapter for the correct syntax of the commands.

a) Create several sample memo files containing status information for different days of the week. You may use the names DAY1.MEMO, DAY2.MEMO and DAY3.MEMO.

Use the CREATE command to create these files and terminate the entry of the data within the CONTROL Z key. Keep the data within the files simple and brief as you will not be able to modify the contents of the file until we consider the editors.

b) Use the DIRECTORY command to list the new files that have been created within the directory.

c) Use the TYPE command to type out the contents of the files just created. Use the asterisk wildcard to select all files with a file name extension of .MEMO.

d) Create a copy of the memo files just created by using the COPY command. You may create the files within your own personal directory using another file name.

Use the DIRECTORY command to view the newly created files. Use the TYPE command to type out the contents of the files and confirm that the same data from the input files is contained within the new files as a result of the COPY.

e) Use the RENAME command to change the file name of one or more of the files to a new name. Again, use both DIRECTORY and TYPE to verify that the file name has been changed.

f) Use the following APPEND command to append all the daily memo files to a single weekly memo file named WEEK_ONE.MEMO. Notice the use of the percent sign (%) wildcard to select the daily memo files. Also, notice the use of the /NEW_VERSION qualifier as there is initially no WEEK_ONE.MEMO file to append to.

```
$ APPEND -
/NEW_VERSION DAY%.MEMO WEEK_ONE.MEMO
```

Again, use the DIRECTORY and TYPE commands to verify that the WEEK_ONE.MEMO file has been created and contains the data from the daily memo files.

g)   Use the DELETE command to delete one or more of the files within your directory. Use the DIRECTORY command to confirm that the files no longer exist.

h)   Create multiple versions of the daily memo files by entering the following command repeatedly. You may use the command line recall feature considered earlier to repeat this command.

```
$ COPY/LOG DAY%.MEMO *
```

Use the DIRECTORY command to verify that multiple versions of these files exist.

i)   Use the PURGE command to delete all the older versions of the files within your directory. Use the DIRECTORY command to confirm that the files have been purged.

j)   Redo some of the above exercises using the generic command qualifiers where applicable. Use the following qualifiers in the manner discussed within this chapter:

/LOG
/CONFIRM
/BEFORE and /SINCE
/EXCLUDE
/OUTPUT

Exercise Answers

Exercise 3a

```
$ CREATE DAY1.MEMO
The status for the first day is that all tasks were
successfully completed. No outstanding items
remain.
^ Z

$ CREATE DAY2.MEMO
The status for the second day is that tasks a, b
and c were completed. Task d remains incomplete and
must be finished at a later time.
^ Z

$ CREATE DAY3.MEMO
The status for the third day is that all tasks were
completed. Task d from the second day was also
completed. All items are finished.
^ Z
```

Exercise 3b

```
$ DIRECTORY
```

Exercise 3c

```
$ TYPE *.MEMO
```

Exercise 3d

```
$ COPY DAY1.MEMO FIRST_DAY.MEMO
$ COPY DAY2.MEMO SECOND_DAY.MEMO
$ COPY DAY3.MEMO THIRD_DAY.MEMO

$ TYPE FIRST_DAY.MEMO
$ TYPE SECOND_DAY.MEMO
$ TYPE THIRD_DAY.MEMO
```

Exercise 3e

```
$ RENAME THIRD_DAY.MEMO LAST_DAY.MEMO
$ DIRECTORY
$ TYPE LAST_DAY.MEMO
```

Exercise 3f

Self-explanatory

Exercise 3g

```
$ DELETE LAST_DAY.MEMO;*
$ DIRECTORY
```

Exercise 3h

Self-explanatory

Exercise 3i

```
$ PURGE
$ DIRECTORY
```

Exercise 3j

```
$ RENAME/LOG/CONFIRM *.MEMO *.STATUS

$ DIRECTORY/OUTPUT=OUT.LIST
$ TYPE OUT.LIST

$ DIRECTORY/BEFORE=01-JAN-1990
$ DIRECTORY/SINCE=01-JAN-1990
```

Chapter Four

Directories

Overview

As we considered during our discussion of the VMS file specification, files are usually stored within various personal directories on storage devices. A single disk drive, for example, may be segregated into a number of different user directories.

Generally, you will be permitted to access only those files which are stored within your own personal directory. There can be numerous exceptions to this statement, however, and our discussion of file protection and security in a later chapter will demonstrate when and how files from other directories may be accessed.

As the amount of work you do with DCL increases, the number of files that may be contained within your personal directory will increase also. Even if you regularly purge older versions of files, you may still, in time, have dozens or even hundreds of different files, containing varying sorts of information, within your directory.

It is at this point that it may be difficult and even quite tedious for you to locate a file you wish to use. The brief explanation of the DIRECTORY command in the previous chapter showed how to list the file names within your directory. However, if hundreds of files are displayed in such a list, the problem of remembering and determining the file name for a specific piece of data becomes quite obvious.

VMS solves this problem with a feature known as subdirectories. You can create any number of subsidiary directories to your main personal directory. For instance, you may wish to create a separate directory for only your memo files, another for data files, and perhaps a third for status reports. The diagram which follows illustrates how such a directory structure might logically appear.

71

Directory / Subdirectory Structure

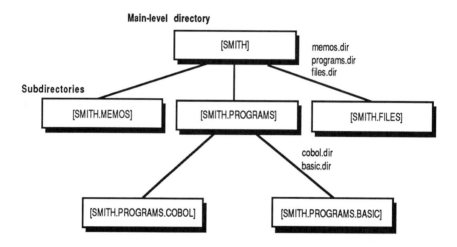

Having created these subdirectories, you may then use the RENAME or COPY commands to move the files stored within the main directory to the newly formed subdirectories. For instance, we may use the RENAME command to move all of the memo files from the main directory for [SMITH] to the subdirectory [SMITH.MEMOS]. Likewise, we may use the RENAME command to move all of the data files that we have created from the main directory to the subdirectory [SMITH.FILES].

You will notice in the above structure that the [SMITH.PROGRAMS] subdirectory has been further divided into additional subdirectories, one for COBOL programs and another for BASIC programs. Similarly, it may prove true in time that the number of memo files within the [SMITH.MEMOS] subdirectory becomes unmanageable, where we have dozens or hundreds of memo files within the subdirectory. It would then be helpful to create subdirectories of the memo subdirectory. We could have a separate subdirectory for January memos named [SMITH.MEMOS.JAN], another for February memos named [SMITH.MEMOS.FEB], and so on.

You do not need any special privileges to create and access subdirectories of your main directory. Further, you may continue to store files within your main directory after you have created subdirectories.

A maximum of eight subdirectory levels may be created. In our sample directory structure that we have displayed, we used a maximum of three subdirectory levels for [SMITH.PROGRAMS.COBOL] and [SMITH.PROGRAMS.BASIC]. While we can divide these subdirectories even further to the maximum limit of eight levels, for practical purposes, however, you may find that a limit of three or four directory levels is adequate. As you can probably imagine, if we created a number of subdirectories, each of which had several subdirectories and levels of subdirectories as well, we could create a directory structure of dozens of subdirectories that becomes almost as unmanageable as our original problem with dozens and dozens of files.

Our sample structure also lists the subdirectory control files that are automatically created when subdirectories are created by the user. These are the files with a file name extension of .DIR. We will consider more detailed information regarding these subdirectory control files later within this chapter.

CREATE/DIRECTORY

Generally, a new user account and corresponding directory will contain only the main directory without any subdirectories. The /DIRECTORY qualifier of the CREATE command creates a subdirectory. Special privileges are required to create a subdirectory for another user's main directory, although none are required for your own area.

The following example creates the sample subdirectories for memos, programs and files within the main directory of SMITH. Notice that after the subdirectories have been created, the subdirectory control files for those subdirectories have also been created and located within the main directory of SMITH.

```
$ CREATE/DIRECTORY [SMITH.MEMOS]
$ CREATE/DIRECTORY [SMITH.PROGRAMS]
$ CREATE/DIRECTORY [SMITH.FILES]
$ DIRECTORY

Directory $DISK1:[SMITH]

FILE1.MEMO;2        FILE2.MEMO;1        FILE3.MEMO;1        FILES.DIR;1
LOGIN.COM;8         MEMOS.DIR;1         NEW.MEMO;2          PROGRAMS.DIR;1
WEEK_ONE.MEMO;5     WEEK_TWO.MEMO;2
```

Note that within a command line the subdirectory names must also be enclosed within square brackets ([ ]). Also, the subdirectory name must be prefaced by the main directory name and separated by a period (.).

Caution

When first creating a subdirectory, a common error is for the user to enter the command CREATE/DIRECTORY [MEMOS] rather than CREATE/DIRECTORY [SMITH.MEMOS]. The incorrect example would create a main directory of [MEMOS] rather than the subdirectory within [SMITH] that we desire. Be certain to create the subdirectories by correctly naming the main directory level first.

Although we have now created the subdirectories, there are no files stored within them at this time. All our memo, program and data files remain stored in the main directory. However, because we have created the subdirectories, we may now use the RENAME command to rename the directory portion of the file specification and thereby move the files to the newly created subdirectories.

In the example below, we will rename all the .MEMO files contained in the default main directory of [SMITH] to the subdirectory of [SMITH.MEMOS]. Thereafter, we use the DIRECTORY command to obtain a listing of the files stored within the subdirectory.

```
$ RENAME *.MEMO [SMITH.MEMOS]*
$ DIRECTORY [SMITH.MEMOS]

Directory $DISK1:[SMITH.MEMOS]

FILE1.MEMO;1          FILE2.MEMO;1          FILE3.MEMO;1          NEW.MEMO;1
WEEK_ONE.MEMO;1       WEEK_TWO.MEMO;1

Total of 6 files.
$
```

We could perform similar commands to rename or copy files from the main directory to the appropriate subdirectories. Thereby, the main directory of [SMITH] will contain the .DIR control files for the subdirectories along with just a few other files. In order to list the memo, program or data files, we may simply use the following commands:

```
$ DIRECTORY  [SMITH.MEMOS]
$ DIRECTORY  [SMITH.PROGRAMS]
$ DIRECTORY  [SMITH.FILES]
```

To take our example further, suppose that there existed so many memo files that even with the creation of a separate subdirectory, the [SMITH.MEMOS] subdirectory contained too many files to be managed easily and we wished to divide the subdirectory into separate structures for the January, February, March, and so on, memos. Or, as in the sample subdirectory structure at the beginning of this chapter, suppose that we had too many program files for the [SMITH.PROGRAMS] subdirectory and wished to divide the subdirectory further into separate structures for the COBOL and BASIC programs.

In the example below, a third subdirectories level is created within the [SMITH.MEMOS] subdirectory. This level contains three separate subdirectories for each of the first three months of the year. Notice that in the [SMITH.MEMOS] subdirectory, there exists the subdirectory control files for the next subdirectory level.

```
$ CREATE/DIRECTORY [SMITH.MEMOS.JAN]
$ CREATE/DIRECTORY [SMITH.MEMOS.FEB]
$ DIRECTORY [SMITH.MEMOS]

Directory $DISK1:[SMITH.MEMOS]

FEB.DIR;1        FILE1.MEMO;1       FILE2.MEMO;1       FILE3.MEMO;1
JAN.DIR;1        NEW.MEMO;1         WEEK_ONE.MEMO;1    WEEK_TWO.MEM

Total of 8 files.
$
```

We can then move out of the memos subdirectory those files created during January and place them in their own directory, the same for February memos, and so on.

```
$ RENAME            -
/SINCE=01-JAN-1989  -
/BEFORE=01-FEB-1989 [SMITH.MEMOS]*.*
[SMITH.MEMOS.JAN]*

$ RENAME            -
/SINCE=01-FEB-1989  -
/BEFORE=01-MAR-1989 [SMITH.MEMOS]*.*
[SMITH.MEMOS.FEB]*
```

We have now created a very segregated directory structure. We may list the files within the third level of subdirectories by naming the subdirectory with the DIRECTORY command.

```
$ DIRECTORY [SMITH.MEMOS.JAN]
$ DIRECTORY [SMITH.MEMOS.FEB]
$ DIRECTORY [SMITH.MEMOS.MAR]
```

Having successfully created the subdirectories and moved the files from the main directory to the appropriate subdirectories, we would likely want to create any new files immediately within the appropriate subdirectory, rather than creating the file within the main directory of [SMITH] and having to rename or copy once again.

This may be done by simply including the directory specification within the file specification. For example, if we were to create a new memo file that belonged in the [SMITH.MEMOS.MAR] subdirectory, we could immediately store the file within the subdirectory with the following CREATE command.

```
$ CREATE [SMITH.MEMOS.MAR]DAY1.MEMO
```

By explicitly stating the directory name within the file specification, the assumed default directory of [SMITH] is not used and the file DAY1.MEMO is immediately stored within the correct subdirectory. If we later wish to access the file with other commands, we would likewise override the default directory of [SMITH] by explicitly naming the subdirectory.

```
$ TYPE [SMITH.MEMOS.JAN]DAY1.MEMO
$ DELETE [SMITH.MEMOS.JAN]DAY2.MEMO;*
$ PURGE [SMITH.MEMOS.FEB]
```

Ellipsis

At this point, you probably see the need for some feature of DCL that would allow us to view and work with files across several subdirectories. If we wanted to view all our memo files in all the monthly directories, we could do so as follows:

```
$ DIRECTORY [SMITH.MEMOS.JAN]
$ DIRECTORY [SMITH.MEMOS.FEB]
$ DIRECTORY [SMITH.MEMOS.MAR]
          .
          .
          .
```

There exists a special wildcard known as the ellipsis (...) that may be used within a directory name as a placeholder for all the subdirectories within the directory stated. For example, if we wanted a directory listing of all subdirectories within the [SMITH.MEMOS] directory structure, we could simply use the following single command:

    $ DIRECTORY [SMITH.MEMOS...]

Similarly we could view all the subdirectories that may exist within the [SMITH.PROGRAMS] directory with the following command.

    $ DIRECTORY [SMITH.PROGRAMS...]

```
Directory $DISK1:[SMITH.MEMOS]

FEB.DIR;1            JAN.DIR;1

Total of 2 files.

Directory $DISK1:[SMITH.MEMOS.FEB]

WEEK_ONE.MEMO;1     WEEK_TWO.MEMO;1

Total of 2 files.

Directory $DISK1:[SMITH.MEMOS.JAN]

FILE1.MEMO;1        FILE2.MEMO;1        FILE3.MEMO;1

Total of 3 files.

Grand total of 4 directories, 11 files.
```

Finally, we could view all the subdirectories, starting from the main directory for SMITH, down to the lowest subdirectory that may exist.

    $ DIRECTORY [SMITH...]

The ellipsis wildcard, as with other wildcards, may be used whenever appropriate in other commands. If we wanted to type out all the files with an extension of .MEMO, regardless of which directory they were in, we could enter the first command below. Or, we could delete all such files with the second command listed below:

    $ TYPE [SMITH...]*.MEMOS;*
    $ DELETE [SMITH...]*.MEMOS;*

SET DEFAULT

Although we have now created a number of subdirectories and moved various files from the main directory into their appropriate subdirectory, VMS will continue to assume that the main directory is our default, unless we specify otherwise. If we were to create a new memo file without explicitly naming the memos subdirectory, as shown below, the new file would be created in the main directory and we would have to use the RENAME command at some later time to move the file to its proper location.

```
$ CREATE DAY5.MEMO
```

As we just considered, the following command would avoid this problem, creating the file and storing it in its proper subdirectory.

```
$ CREATE [SMITH.MEMO.MAR]DAY5.MEMO
```

As you can imagine, if we were to work with a series of files stored within the March subdirectory, it would be tiresome to always preface every file specification with the lengthy subdirectory name. To avoid this problem, VMS allows you to change the default directory that it will assume when a directory is not explicitly stated. Once this is done, the newly named subdirectory is now the default, and access to the main directory (or another subdirectory) can be done only if the default is changed or the main directory is explicitly stated.

In the following example, the user enters the SET DEFAULT command to change the default directory that VMS will assume when none has been explicitly stated. Rather than assuming [SMITH] as the directory, VMS and all DCL commands will now assume the directory of [SMITH.MEMOS.JAN], unless another directory is explicitly stated within the command.

The DEFAULT option of the SHOW command displays the current default directory.

```
$ SET DEFAULT [SMITH.MEMOS.JAN]
$ SHOW DEFAULT
  $DISK1:[SMITH.MEMOS.JAN]
```

All subsequent commands now assume the default directory [SMITH.MEMOS.JAN]. Note the assumed default below when the DIRECTORY command is used without naming any specific directory.

```
$ DIRECTORY

Directory $DISK1:[SMITH.MEMOS.JAN]

FILE1.MEMO;1          FILE2.MEMO;1          FILE3.MEMO;1

Total of 3 files.
$
```

When a new process is started, the initial default directory, usually the main directory, is reset. The user must again change the default with the SET DEFAULT command.

Directory Specification

As you are now aware, the directory assumed by VMS is the current default, unless specified otherwise. When specifying a directory explicitly, you have the option of using ellipsis (...) to include a number of directory levels.

There are additional features which you can use when specifying a directory. The dash [-] refers to the directory that exists one level higher than the current default. For example, if our current default were [SMITH.MEMOS.JAN] and we wished to refer to [SMITH.MEMOS] in a command, we could use the dash in place of the actual specification, as follows:

```
$ DIRECTORY [-]

$ TYPE [-]SAMPLE_FILE.DATA
```

Conversely, when referring to a subdirectory one level lower than the current default, it is not necessary to include the current default within the brackets. If our default were now [SMITH.MEMOS] and we wanted to specify the [SMITH.MEMOS.FEB] subdirectory for various DCL commands, we could simply enter the following:

```
$ DIRECTORY [.FEB]

$ TYPE [.FEB]NEW_FILE.MEMO
```

By including the period at the beginning, we indicate a subdirectory. However, by not specifying the main-level directory, the current default is assumed.

Note

Be sure that you do not omit the period and simply specify the directory as [FEB]. This would indicate a main-level directory of [FEB], which, of course, does not exist.

Also, when you imply a higher-level directory by simply specifying the period before the subdirectory, you must be aware of what the current default is. For example, suppose that we assumed that our current default was the main directory of [SMITH] and we entered the command SET DEFAULT [.MEMOS]. If however, we had already set our default to the memos subdirectory, this command would actually set our default to [SMITH.MEMOS.MEMOS], which again does not exist.

DIRECTORY

We briefly considered this command earlier. There are a number of additional options which exist with this command that are very helpful. Regardless of the qualifiers or options selected, the DIRECTORY command will work with our default main directory unless we specify another main directory or subdirectory.

The /BEFORE and /SINCE qualifiers that we are familiar with from other commands can also be used to limit the files displayed as part of the directory listing. Note the following commands:

```
$ DIRECTORY/BEFORE=TODAY

$ DIRECTORY/SINCE=01-JAN-1989 [SMITH.MEMOS...]
```

We can request that the files be listed in a single column (or more), rather than across the entire terminal screen.

```
$ DIRECTORY/COLUMN=1

Directory $DISK1:[SMITH]

FILES.DIR;1
LOGIN.COM;8
MEMOS.DIR;1
PROGRAMS.DIR;1

Total of 4 files.
$
```

In addition to selecting files based upon their creation or modification date, we may select files based upon their size (in terms of 512 character disk blocks). In the first example below, we select files between 0 and 10 blocks large. In the next, we select files between 100 and 1000 blocks large.

```
$ DIRECTORY -
/SELECT=SIZE=(MIN=0,MAX=10)  [SMITH.MEMOS.JAN]

$ DIRECTORY -
/SELECT=SIZE=(MIN=100,MAX=1000) [SMITH...]
```

There are other qualifiers which display important information about a file in addition to just simply the file name and version number. When selecting files for different operations based upon their creation date, we obviously need to know what the creation date is for various files. Or, when selecting files based upon their size, we need to know the sizes of the files. This information is available with the /DATE and /SIZE qualifiers of the DIRECTORY command.

```
$ SET DEFAULT [SMITH.MEMOS.JAN]
$ DIRECTORY/SIZE/DATE

Directory $DISK1:[SMITH.MEMOS.JAN]

FILE1.MEMO;1              9   30-AUG-1989 09:23
FILE2.MEMO;1             1   30-AUG-1989 09:23
FILE3.MEMO;1             1   30-AUG-1989 09:24
```

Using the /FULL qualifier, we can display all the information pertaining to a file.

```
$ DIRECTORY/FULL FILE1.MEMO

Directory $DISK1:[SMITH.MEMOS.JAN]

FILE1.MEMO;1                File ID:  (443,40,0)
Size:             9/10     Owner:    [400,1]
Created:   30-AUG-1989 09:23  Revised:  30-AUG-1989 14:20 (14)
Expires:    <None specified>  Backup:    <No backup recorded>
File organization:  Sequential
File attributes:    Allocation: 10, Extend: 0, Global buffer count: 0
                    No version limit
Record format:      Variable length, maximum 50 bytes
Record attributes:  Carriage return carriage control
Journaling enabled: None
File protection:    System:RWED, Owner:RWED, Group:RE, World:
Access Cntrl List:  None

Total of 1 file, 9/10 blocks.
$
```

Chapter 4 Exercises

Within the exercises for this chapter, we will attempt the following:

- Create subdirectories with the CREATE/DIRECTORY command.

- Move existing files to the subdirectories and create new files within the subdirectories.

- Change the assumed default directory with the SET DEFAULT command.

- Use the new qualifiers and other options available with the DIRECTORY command.

Exercise 1
CREATE/DIRECTORY

a) Use the SHOW DEFAULT and the DIRECTORY command to view your initial default-level directory on your account, which is usually the top-level directory.

b) Use the CREATE/DIRECTORY command to develop a subdirectory structure for your main directory. You may use any subdirectories that you wish, but create the following structure as a minimum. (Obviously, you must insert your own main directory level name in place of [SMITH] as shown within our examples here.

- A subdirectory of [.MEMOS] within your main-level directory

- Subdirectories of [.JAN], [.FEB] and [.MAR] within the [.MEMOS] subdirectory

c) After creating the subdirectories, use the DIRECTORY command to view the subdirectory control files within the higher-level directories.

Exercise 2
Using Subdirectories

a) Use the RENAME command to move certain files from the top-level directory to the appropriate subdirectory. Use the DIRECTORY command to list the files within the subdirectories.

b) Include the subdirectory specification with the CREATE command to create a new file immediately within the appropriate subdirectory. Include the subdirectory specification with the TYPE command to type out the contents of the files from their new subdirectory location.

Exercise 3
SET DEFAULT

a) Change the default directory to one of the subdirectories with the SET DEFAULT command.

b) Note the changed default directory with the SHOW DEFAULT and DIRECTORY commands. Also note that all DCL file maintenance commands used now assume the new default directory.

Exercise 4
DIRECTORY Specification and Qualifiers

a) Use the ellipsis (...) and dash (-) within the DIRECTORY command to list subdirectories levels lower and higher than the current default.

b) Use the new qualifiers introduced for the DIRECTORY command, including the following:

- /COLUMNS
- /SELECT=SIZE
- /DATE
- /SIZE
- /FULL

Exercise Answers

Exercise 1a

Self-explanatory

Exercise 1b

```
$ CREATE/DIRECTORY [SMITH.MEMOS]
$ CREATE/DIRECTORY [SMITH.MEMOS.JAN]
$ CREATE/DIRECTORY [SMITH.MEMOS.FEB]
$ CREATE/DIRECTORY [SMITH.MEMOS.MAR]
```

Exercise 1c

```
$ DIRECTORY [SMITH]*.DIR
$ DIRECTORY [SMITH.MEMOS]*.DIR
```

Exercise 2a

```
$ RENAME [SMITH]DAY%.MEMO [SMITH.MEMOS]*
$ DIRECTORY [SMITH]
$ DIRECTORY [SMITH.MEMOS]
```

Exercise 2b

```
$ CREATE [SMITH.MEMOS.JAN]JANUARY.STATUS
This is a summary status report for the month of
January...
^ Z

$ TYPE [SMITH.MEMOS.JAN]JANUARY.STATUS
```

Exercise 3a

```
$ SET DEFAULT [SMITH.MEMOS.JAN]
```

Exercise 3b

```
$ SHOW DEFAULT
$ DIRECTORY
$ TYPE JANUARY.STATUS
```

Exercise 4a

```
$ SET DEFAULT [SMITH]
$ DIRECTORY [SMITH...]
$ DIRECTORY [SMITH.MEMOS...]

$ SET DEFAULT [SMITH.MEMOS]
$ DIRECTORY [-]
```

Exercise 4b

```
$ DIRECTORY/COLUMNS=1
$ DIRECTORY/SELECT=SIZE
$ DIRECTORY/DATE
$ DIRECTORY/SIZE
$ DIRECTORY/FULL
```

Chapter Five

File Protection and Control

Overview

The file maintenance commands that we have considered create or alter data stored within user files. This chapter describes controlling the characteristics of the files and includes the following topics:

- File protection or security
- File version limits
- Other file control characteristics

File Protection Overview

The primary method of file protection involves the User Identification Code (UIC). For each user (that is, user name) authorized to log on to the VAX, the system manager creates a user profile. That profile includes such items as the user name, password, various resource allocations and the UIC. When a user logs in with a certain user name, the process is automatically assigned the corresponding UIC as stated by the system manager within the user profile.

The UIC is comprised of two components, the group code and the individual code. These codes may be either numeric or alphabetic. Thus, the UIC serves to identify a user with a unique identification code for security purposes and also to classify that user with others in a UIC group. The following sample UICs show several users within the AP (accounts payable) or GL (general ledger) groups, but with each having his or her own individual code.

```
[AP,  SMITH]
[AP,  JONES]
[GL,  WILSON]
[GL,  MARINO]
```

Note once again our sample display from the SHOW PROCESS command and see that the process has been assigned a UIC group code of GUEST and an individual code of SMITH.

```
$ SHOW PROCESS

27-AUG-1989 21:39:32.88   VTA1:              User: SMITH
Pid: 00000029   Proc. name: SMITH X5522     UIC: [GUEST,SMITH]
Priority:   4   Default file spec: $DISK1:[SMITH]

Devices allocated: VTA1:
$
```

Whenever a file is created it is also assigned a UIC code at that time. By default, the file receives the same UIC as the process that created it. Whenever any process attempts to access that file after its creation, VMS matches the UIC code of the inquiring process with the UIC of the file, and based on the result of the match, determines the allowed access.

During the UIC matching between the inquiring process and the file, the following results may occur:

- The inquiring process and the file have identical UICs, that is, both the group and the individual codes of the process and the file are the same. As this most likely indicates that the inquiring user actually created the file, the process is considered to be the OWNER.

- The inquiring process and the file have matching group numbers or names within the UIC, although the individual codes do not match. Thus, the inquiring process is not designated as the owner, but is considered to be within the same GROUP.

- The inquiring process and the file have neither identical group codes nor individual codes. The process is not designated as either the owner or a group user, but is considered to be within the WORLD.

- As an exception to the above, UICs that have a group code that identifies them as a system user are recognized as a special SYSTEM process.

For each of the four classes of processes, OWNER, GROUP, WORLD and SYSTEM, there is a separate set of file protections that are provided. The list of file protections that may be made available to any of the classes of processes are as follows:

- R or READ protection. The inquiring process is permitted to read the file, including copying the file into its own directory.

- W or WRITE protection. The inquiring process is permitted to add or modify data within the file.

- D or DELETE protection. The inquiring process is permitted to delete the file.

- E or EXECUTE protection. If the file is either a command procedure or an executable program, the inquiring process is permitted to run or execute the file.

- The owner process also implicitly has a control protection, which means that this process may alter the file protections granted for itself and all other processes.

DIRECTORY/PROTECTION/OWNER
DIRECTORY/SECURITY

Using the rules described above, we can anticipate the file protections that will be granted a process by examining the owner UIC of a file and comparing it against the UIC of an inquiring process and classifying the user as an owner, or as a group, world or system user. Next we can examine the specific protections permitted such a user. We have already seen that the SHOW PROCESS command displays the UIC of a process. Qualifiers of the DIRECTORY command will list the owner UIC and the protections for a file.

The /OWNER qualifier of the DIRECTORY command lists the owner UIC of the file, which is very likely the same UIC as the process that created the file (for example, the OWNER).

```
$ DIRECTORY/OWNER

Directory $DISK1:[SMITH.MEMOS.JAN]

FILE1.MEMO;1          [GUEST,SMITH]
FILE2.MEMO;1          [GUEST,SMITH]
FILE3.MEMO;1          [GUEST,SMITH]

Total of 3 files.
$
```

The /PROTECTION qualifier of the DIRECTORY command lists the file protections provided for each of the four classes of processes. The protections are listed in the order of SYSTEM, OWNER, GROUP, WORLD. In our example listing of the files within the [SMITH.MEMOS.JAN] subdirectory, note that the fourth column for world users is blank, indicating that no access at all is permitted such users.

```
$ DIRECTORY/PROTECTION

Directory $DISK1:[SMITH.MEMOS.JAN]

FILE1.MEMO;1          (RWED,RWED,RE,)
FILE2.MEMO;1          (RWED,RWED,RE,)
FILE3.MEMO;1          (RWED,RWED,RE,)

Total of 3 files.
$
```

The DIRECTORY/SECURITY command will list both the owner UIC and the authorized file protections, or all security information for the file.

```
$ DIRECTORY/SECURITY

Directory $DISK1:[SMITH.MEMOS.JAN]

FILE1.MEMO;1       [GUEST,SMITH]         (RWED,RWED,RE,R)
FILE2.MEMO;1       [GUEST,SMITH]         (RWED,RWED,RE,R)
FILE3.MEMO;1       [GUEST,SMITH]         (RWED,RWED,RE,R)

Total of 3 files.
$
```

And as we have seen before, the DIRECTORY/FULL command will list all information regarding a file, including all the security information.

SET FILE/PROTECTION

The file protection for the four classes of users may be altered for one or more files with the PROTECTION qualifier of the SET FILE command. The following example gives all access to all classes of users for a specific file. The order in which the protections are specified is not important as long as the syntax follows the format shown.

```
$ SET FILE/PROTECTION=(SYSTEM:RWED,OWNER:RWED, -
GROUP:RWED,WORLD:RWED) FILE1.MEMO
```

The next example grants only certain protections to GROUP and WORLD users. Note the allowed abbreviation for the classes of users. As with any other file maintenance or control command, wildcards may be used in place of a single file name.

```
$ SET FILE/PROTECTION=(S:RWED,O:RWED, -
G:RE,W:R) *.*;*
```

Users may be denied all protections by specifying their identifier without any protection code or separating colon (:). The following example denies protections to all users except the owner, who retains all protections.

```
$ SET FILE/PROTECTION=(S,O:RWED,G,W) *.*;*
```

In our prior example of the file protections granted, world users had no access at all. The following command grants read access to world users, while leaving the protections for the other classes of users intact.

```
$ SET FILE/PROTECTION=(WORLD:R) *.*;*
$ DIRECTORY/PROTECTION

Directory $DISK1:[SMITH.MEMOS.JAN]

FILE1.MEMO;1          (RWED,RWED,RE,R)
FILE2.MEMO;1          (RWED,RWED,RE,R)
FILE3.MEMO;1          (RWED,RWED,RE,R)

Total of 3 files.
$
```

SET PROTECTION/DEFAULT

While the above examples illustrate the manner in which protections can be changed for an existing file, we have not considered how the original protections are allocated when the file is first created.

The SHOW PROTECTION command lists the default file access protections that are in effect for any files created for your process. As we observe the output from the command, we can see why the memo files within the subdirectory initially had no access granted to world users.

```
$ SHOW PROTECTION
  SYSTEM=RWE, OWNER=RWED, GROUP=RE, WORLD=NO ACCESS
$
```

The default protection initially assigned files created by the process may be changed with the SET PROTECTION/DEFAULT command. Note the following change to the default protection which grants world users read access by default. All files created henceforth by the process will be granted this protection.

```
$ SET PROTECTION=(SYSTEM:RWE,OWNER:RWED,GROUP:RE,WORLD:R)/DEFAULT
$ SHOW PROTECTION
  SYSTEM=RWE, OWNER=RWED, GROUP=RE, WORLD=R
$
```

The changed default protection is valid only for the duration of the process and will revert back to the original default when a new login session is started. Include the command within the LOGIN.COM file to permanently alter the default file protection.

Note

The SET PROTECTION/DEFAULT command will alter the protection for newly created files only. File privileges for existing files are not changed by this command. Use the SET FILE/PROTECTION command, as just described within this section, to alter the file protections for existing files.

SET FILE/VERSION_LIMIT

By default, DCL will retain virtually an indefinite number of versions (actually 32,767) of files as they are changed. This provides users with the opportunity to examine prior file versions and use these as desired. The obvious disadvantage to this feature, though, is the excess disk space consumed, especially if the older versions are not always needed.

While the PURGE command will delete older versions of a file, the user must remember to use this command from time to time.

DCL permits a version limit to be imposed upon files, and this may be stated on a file-by-file basis, with unique version limits for each file depending upon the need. Thus, when a file is modified and a new version created, should the new version result in the version limit being exceeded, the oldest version is automatically deleted. The end result is that only the number of versions indicated by the version limit are actually retained.

It is important to understand that although a version limit is imposed upon a file, the file may still be modified and a new version will still be created. DCL simply deletes the oldest version of the file and continues to retain the number of versions stated by the limit.

The following command changes the version limit of all files within the current default directory from the default limit of an infinite number of versions to only five.

```
$ SET FILE/VERSION_LIMIT=5 *.*;*
```

We may determine the current version limit for a file by using the DIRECTORY/FULL command.

Note

When the version limit for a file is reduced below the number of versions currently stored on disk, the SET FILE/VERSION_LIMIT command will not automatically delete the excess versions. The command simply changes the version limit. In this case, the user must manually use the PURGE command to delete the excess versions. Thereafter, the reduced version limit will be correctly maintained.

SET DIRECTORY/VERSION_LIMIT

Similar to a change in file protections, changes to a file's version limit do not alter the default version limit initially imposed upon new files. This is done with the SET DIRECTORY/VERSION_LIMIT command.

Unlike default file protections, which are assigned all files created by a process, the default version limit is different depending upon which directory or subdirectory a file is created in.

The following command sets the default version limit to be assigned newly created files to five. However, this is only done for files created within the [SMITH.MEMOS.JAN] subdirectory. All other subdirectories retain their original version limit.

```
$ SET DIRECTORY/VERSION_LIMIT=5 [SMITH.MEMOS.JAN]
```

We could change the version limits for all subdirectories with a single command by including the ellipsis within the subdirectory specification.

Once the version limit for a subdirectory has been changed, it is a permanent change that is not lost when the process terminates. The next session will have the same version limit for the subdirectory.

Using the series of commands below, we could alter the version limits for all files within all subdirectories, and do the same for all newly created files.

```
$ SET DIRECTORY/VERSION_LIMIT=5 [SMITH...]
$ SET FILE/VERSION_LIMIT=5 [SMITH...]*.*;*
$ PURGE
```

SET FILE/OWNER_UIC
SET FILE/ERASE_ON_DELETE

There are several additional file attributes that may be altered with qualifiers of the SET FILE command. We will briefly consider these within this section.

As mentioned, the owner UIC initially assigned a file is the same as the UIC of the process that created the file. This may be changed with the following command. Special process privileges are required in order to perform this command.

```
$ SET FILE/OWNER_UIC=[GUEST,JONES] FILE1.MEMO;*
```

The DELETE command included the /ERASE qualifier which physically destroyed the data contained in the file being deleted. We may establish ERASE as an attribute for the file so that any time a version of the file is deleted within either the DELETE or PURGE commands, the /ERASE qualifier is automatically applied.

```
$ SET FILE/ERASE_ON_DELETE FILE1.MEMO;*
```

Chapter 5 Exercises

With the exercises within this chapter, you will attempt the following:

- Change the default file protections assigned new files.
- Change the file protections of existing files.
- Change the default version limit assigned new files.
- Change the version limit of existing files.

Exercise 1
File Protections

a) Examine your own process UIC with the SHOW PROCESS command.

b) Examine the current default file protections assigned to new files with the SHOW PROTECTION command.

c) Use any of the following qualifiers of the DIRECTORY command to observe that the process UIC and default file protections have been assigned to files you have already created.

- DIRECTORY/OWNER
- DIRECTORY/PROTECTION
- DIRECTORY/SECURITY
- DIRECTORY/FULL

d) Use the SET PROTECTION/DEFAULT command to change the default protection assigned new files. Then create a new file using the CREATE command and check that the new default protection was correctly assigned to the new file by using the DIRECTORY command qualifiers as stated above.

e) Change the protection for an existing file by using the SET FILE/PROTECTION command. Deny your own process (the owner) read access and then attempt to read the file with the TYPE command. Also view the changed protection with the DIRECTORY command qualifiers.

Exercise 2
File Versions

a) Use the DIRECTORY/FULL command to observe the current default version limit for the existing files you have created.

b) Change the default version limit assigned files within a certain subdirectory by using the SET DIRECTORY/VERSION_LIMIT command. Create a new file within that subdirectory and observe the change with the DIRECTORY/FULL command.

c) Change the version limit assigned for a specific file to only two versions by using the SET FILE/VERSION_LIMIT command and verify the change to the file with the DIRECTORY/FULL command. Use the PURGE command to delete all older versions of the file.

d) Using either the COPY or CREATE commands as described in earlier chapters, create additional versions of the same file. Use the DIRECTORY/BRIEF command to observe that only the correct number of versions are actually being retained.

Exercise Answers

Exercise 1a-1c

Self-explanatory

Exercise 1d

```
$ SET PROTECTION=(S,O:RWED,G,W)/DEFAULT
$ CREATE TEST_PROTECTION.FILE
Junk file to test the protection code on new file
^ Z
$ DIRECTORY/PROTECTION
```

Exercise 1e

```
$ SET FILE/PROTECTION= -
(S,O:D,G,W)  TEST_PROTECTION.FILE
$ DIRECTORY/PROTECTION TEST_PROTECTION.FILE
$ TYPE TEST_PROTECTION.FILE
```

Exercise 2a

```
$ DIRECTORY/FULL [SMITH.MEMOS.JAN]
```

Exercise 2b

```
$ SET DIRECTORY/VERSION_LIMIT=2 [SMITH.MEMOS.JAN]
$ CREATE [SMITH.MEMOS.JAN]TEST_VERSIONS.FILE
Second junk file; test version limit assigned file
^ Z
$ DIRECTORY -
/FULL [SMITH.MEMOS.JAN]TEST_VERSIONS.FILE
```

Exercise 2c

```
$ SET FILE/VERSION_LIMIT=2 [SMITH]DAY1.MEMO
$ DIRECTORY/FULL [SMITH]DAY1.MEMO
$ PURGE [SMITH]DAY1.MEMO
```

Exercised 2d

```
$ CREATE [SMITH]DAY1.MEMO
another version...
^ Z

$ CREATE [SMITH]DAY1.MEMO
another version...
^ Z

$ CREATE [SMITH]DAY1.MEMO
another version...
^ Z

$ DIRECTORY/BRIEF [SMITH]DAY1.MEMO
```

Chapter Six

Logical Names and Symbols

Overview

Logical names and symbols are somewhat similar in their general purpose. Both logical names and symbols provide the user with the ability to define alias names for certain portions of the DCL command string. While their general purpose is somewhat the same, the two should not be confused, as their specific purpose and function are very different.

The definition of a logical name allows the user to define an alias name for various VMS items, most typically, a file name or a portion of a file name specification. Having defined the alias, or logical name, for a file specification, you may then use the logical name interchangeably with the physical file specification. While there are other uses of logical names, such as for queue names, they are most often used to represent a file specification.

Symbols also have several uses. Perhaps the most common, though, is to allow the user to define a foreign command. Using a symbol, the user may define an alias name, or foreign command name, as an equivalent to an actual DCL verb and qualifiers. Having defined such a symbol or foreign command, the user may then use the symbol name interchangeably with the actual DCL verb and qualifier.

It is important to remember that both user-defined logical names and symbols are valid only for the current user session. Once the user logs off, and the user process is deleted, any user-defined logical names and symbols are lost. These may be automatically redefined during the next user session, however, as part of the login command procedure.

The sections that follow within this chapter describe the specific manner in which both logical names and symbols are defined and maintained.

We will first consider these topics for logical names:

- Logical name definition

- Logical name maintenance

- Logical name tables

We will then consider these topics for symbols:

- Symbol definition

- Symbol maintenance

Logical Name Definition

As already discussed, a physical VMS file specification, or a portion thereof, may be equated to a VMS logical name. Once the logical name has been defined, the logical name may be used in place of the actual physical name.

There are two main benefits to defining and subsequently using logical names rather than physical file specifications. While defining logical names is not mandatory, it is strongly encouraged.

The first benefit is ease of use. As we have already considered, the VMS file specification can be quite lengthy and has several precise rules as to how it must be specified. Such a specification may be equated to a logical name of your own choice and need not have the special characters and other grammatical rules of a physical name. This simpler, logical name of your own choice may then be used in place of the physical name.

For example, note the following use of the DIRECTORY command with the physical specification of the subdirectory.

```
$ DIRECTORY [SMITH.MEMOS.JAN]

Directory $DISK1:[SMITH.MEMOS.JAN]

FILE1.MEMO;1          FILE2.MEMO;1          FILE3.MEMO;1

Total of 3 files.
```

By defining a logical name JAN and equating it to the physical name, the logical name may be used instead of the physical name and with greater ease and familiarity to the user.

Notice how this same command is performed using the more convenient logical name JAN, but achieving the same results.

```
$ DEFINE JAN "[SMITH.MEMOS.JAN]"
$ DIRECTORY JAN

Directory $DISK1:[SMITH.MEMOS.JAN]

FILE1.MEMO;1          FILE2.MEMO;1          FILE3.MEMO;1
```

The following rules pertain to the use of the DEFINE command to establish a
logical name.

- The first parameter states the logical name desired by the user. The
  name may be no more than 255 characters in length.

- The second parameter states the physical specification to be equated
  to the logical name. All the standard rules for using physical
  specifications must be observed. While it is not always required, it
  is good practice to include the second parameter within quotes.

We may also include the logical name JAN within a physical file specification.
If we wanted to type out the file FILE1.MEMO stored within the subdirectory,
we could use the logical name for the directory portion of the file specification.
Or we could use the logical name with the DELETE command, and so on.

```
$ TYPE  JAN:FILE1.MEMO

$ DELETE  JAN:FILE1.MEMO;*
```

The colon (:) is required to separate the logical name JAN from the physical
name FILE1.MEMO.

Consider the next example where a logical name is used to define the full file
specification, rather than just the directory.

```
$ DEFINE F1 "[SMITH.MEMOS.JAN]FILE1.MEMO"
$ TYPE F1
This is data contained within a brief file called FILE1.MEMO.
$
```

Once a logical name has been defined for a certain file specification, the
definition may be overridden simply by using the same logical name with a new
equivalence or physical name. We could modify the logical name F1 to represent
the first version of FILE1.MEMO. Thereafter, any use of the logical name F1
will be translated to version 1.

```
$ DEFINE F1 "[SMITH.MEMOS.JAN]FILE1.MEMO;1"
%DCL-I-SUPERSEDE, previous value of F1 has been superseded
$
```

An information message informing the user that the logical name was redefined is automatically generated as we can see. This may be suppressed with the /NOLOG qualifier.

The second, and perhaps more important benefit to using logical names pertains to a concept called device independence. By using logical names throughout an application or user session, rather than physical names, the physical location of a file and its corresponding logical name definition may be changed without any user knowledge or concern. Users simply continue to refer to the logical name and its current physical equivalence.

To illustrate, suppose that there were dozens of command procedures, programs and interactive users who accessed a file stored at the following location:

- Node name of EARTH::
- Disk name of DUA0:
- Directory name of [SMITH.MEMOS.JAN]
- File name of FILE1.MEMO

These command procedures, programs, etc., could use the full physical name as follows:

```
$ DIRECTORY -
  EARTH::DUA0:[SMITH.MEMOS.JAN]FILE1.MEMO
```

Assume that the interactive users, command procedures and application programs all refer to the file by means of its physical file name. Should the data file need to be moved to another VAX, disk drive or disk directory, every reference by users, command procedures and programs needs to be changed to reflect the new physical location. This could involve changes to hundreds of references to the physical specification within dozens of command procedures and programs.

We could solve this problem by defining a logical name for each portion of the file specification. Thereafter, all command procedures and programs would refer to the appropriate logical name rather than the physical name. In our example, we will use the following logical names:

- NODE as a logical name for the VAX node name EARTH::.

- DISK as a logical name for the disk DUA0: on the VAX node

EARTH::.

- ACCOUNT as a logical name for the user directory [SMITH.MEMOS.JAN] stored on the disk DUA0: and the VAX node EARTH::.

- FILE as the logical name for the file FILE1.MEMO stored in the above location.

The following shows the definition of the logical name FILE for our target file. The logical name FILE itself refers to another logical name within its definition, namely ACCOUNT. This logical name, in turn, refers to the logical name for the disk, and so on.

```
$ DEFINE NODE "EARTH::"
$ DEFINE DISK "NODE::DUA0:"
$ DEFINE ACCOUNT "DISK:[SMITH.MEMOS.JAN]"
$ DEFINE FILE "ACCOUNT:FILE1.MEMO"
```

Command procedures and programs no longer should refer to the physical name for the file but rather the logical name FILE with its references to other logical names.

```
$ DIRECTORY FILE

Directory EARTH::DUA0:[SMITH.MEMOS.JAN]

FILE1.MEMO;2        FILE1.MEMO;1

Total of 2 files.
```

In the event the data file was moved to another VAX, such as VAX2::, only the logical name NODE need be changed. The logical name FILE indirectly refers to the logical name and all command procedures and programs continue to use the same logical name, with no changes at all.

```
$ DEFINE NODE "VAX2::"

$ DIRECTORY FILE
```

Logical Name Maintenance

The maintenance of logical names consists of the following functions:

- Displaying the current definition of one or all logical names.

- Changing the current definition for a logical name.

- Deleting a logical name definition.

The current definition of a logical name may be viewed with the SHOW LOGICAL command and the identification of a logical name.

```
$ SHOW LOGICAL NODE
  "NODE" = "EARTH::" (LNM$PROCESS_TABLE)
$ SHOW LOGICAL DISK
  "DISK" = "NODE::DUA0:" (LNM$PROCESS_TABLE)
```

Using the SHOW LOGICAL command without identifying a specific logical name will display all the logical names defined, including numerous logical names automatically defined by VMS and not the user. Logical names are displayed in alphabetical order, not the order in which they were defined.

```
$ SHOW LOGICAL

(LNM$PROCESS_TABLE)

  "ACCOUNT" = "DISK:[SMITH.MEMOS.JAN]"
  "DISK" = "NODE::DUA0:"
  "FILE" = "ACCOUNT:FILE1.MEMO"
  "NODE" = "EARTH::"
  "SYS$COMMAND" = "_VTA1:"
  "SYS$DISK" = "$DISK1:"
  "SYS$ERROR" = "_VTA1:"
  "SYS$INPUT" = "_VTA1:"
  "SYS$OUTPUT" [super] = "_VTA1:"
  "SYS$OUTPUT" [exec] = "_VTA1:"
  "TT" = "VTA1:"
```

As already mentioned, the equivalence definition or physical specification for a logical name may be changed simply by using the same logical name with a different physical name as part of the DEFINE verb.

Also as described earlier, all user-defined logical names are automatically deleted when the user logs off and the process terminates. Within an interactive session though, one or all logical names may be immediately deleted.

```
$ DEASSIGN FILE

$ DEASSIGN/ALL
```

Logical Name Tables

There are basically two different categories of logical names, those that are defined by users for their personal use and those that are defined by group or system managers for many users. The extent to which a logical name affects one or more users is determined by which logical name table a logical name is defined in. The following list identifies the default logical name tables within VMS:

- LNM$PROCESS

- LNM$JOB

- LNM$GROUP

- LNM$SYSTEM

Logical name tables are segments of memory that are used to store the logical name definitions. By default, logical names defined by a user for their process are stored within the LNM$PROCESS table.

Each process has a portion of its memory allocated for the LNM$PROCESS table. Logical names which are inserted into the LNM$PROCESS table affect only that process, that is, the user's current session. (It is for this reason that logical name definitions are lost when the process is deleted as part of the logout operation.)

A single user may initiate several subprocesses. Each subprocess, being a separate process, has its own LNM$PROCESS table. However, all subprocesses and the main process share a single logical name table called LNM$JOB. Thus, a user who wishes to define a logical name and have it effective for the main process and all subprocesses would do so by inserting the logical name within the LNM$JOB table. This may be done as follows:

```
$ DEFINE/TABLE=LNM$JOB FILE "FILE1.MEMO;1"
```

Within the chapter for file protection we considered the UIC assigned to each user. By means of the UIC group code, the system manager categorizes various users as being within the same group. All processes within a group, in addition to their own LNM$PROCESS and LNM$JOB tables, share a single LNM$GROUP table. Thus, if a logical name is defined within the LNM$GROUP table, it is available for use by all processes within that group (that is, all processes which share the same UIC group code), even though they may not have defined any logical names of their own within their own tables. Logical names are inserted within the group table as follows:

```
$ DEFINE/TABLE=LNM$GROUP FILE "FILE1.MEMO;1"
```

Finally, all users on the system, regardless of their group UIC code, share a single system-wide logical name table called LNM$SYSTEM. Logical names that are inserted into the system table are effective for all users on the system. System-wide logical names may be defined in a similar manner as above simply by naming the LNM$SYSTEM table as the logical name table to be used.

```
$ DEFINE/TABLE=LNM$SYSTEM FILE "FILE1.MEMO;1"
```

The SHOW LOGICAL command described in the previous section to list all logical names lists the names within all tables. To list logical names from a specific table, the following command and qualifier are required.

```
$ SHOW LOGICAL/TABLE=LNM$GROUP
```

You will notice that in each of the tables displayed, there are a number of system-defined logical names created by VMS, in addition to any that you may define.

Since neither the LNM$SYSTEM table nor the LNM$GROUP tables apply to a single user or process but to multiple processes and users, these tables do not need to be redefined whenever any user logs off and his process terminates. These tables remain intact as long as the system is up. (Should the system be shut down and thereafter be restarted, these logical name tables must be reconstructed as part of the start up procedure, similar to the login procedure that is executed whenever a user session starts up).

Also, due to the fact that system memory is consumed by these tables and many users are affected by such logical names, special privileges are needed to insert logical names within the group or system tables. No special privileges are needed to insert logical names within the process or job tables.

Symbol Definition

Symbols permit the user to define a symbolic command, that is, an alias name for a valid DCL verb and optional qualifiers. Thus, the symbolic command name may be used in place of the actual DCL verb and qualifiers.

The following example creates a symbolic command LIST, which equates to the DCL verb DIRECTORY along with several qualifiers.

```
$ LIST = "DIRECTORY/SIZE/DATE/PROTECTION"
```

The symbol LIST may then be used in place of the DCL command.

```
$ LIST

Directory $DISK1:[SMITH.MEMOS.JAN]

FILE1.MEMO;2           1  31-AUG-1989 10:27  (RWED,RWED,RE,R)
FILE1.MEMO;1           9  30-AUG-1989 09:23  (RWED,RWED,RE,R)
FILE2.MEMO;1           1  30-AUG-1989 09:23  (RWED,RWED,RE,R)
FILE3.MEMO;1           1  30-AUG-1989 09:24  (RWED,RWED,RE,R)

Total of 4 files, 12 blocks.
```

The symbol name may be no longer than 255 characters. In place of the required quotation marks that surround the actual DCL command string, the use of the colon as follows implies the quotation marks:

```
$ LIST:= DIRECTORY/SIZE/DATE/PROTECTION
```

Symbols are stored within a portion of user memory known as the symbol tables. Each process has a local and a global table. Local symbols are effective for only the current command level and any lower command level. Global symbols are effective for all command levels for a process. While command levels are discussed in further detail in Chapter 12, "Command Procedures," let us state that global symbols are effective everywhere within a user process, whereas local symbols are not. Therefore, global symbols should generally be used.

Symbols are inserted into the local symbol table when they are defined with a single equal sign. Global symbols are defined with a double equal sign. The following example defines the symbol LIST once again, but this time as a global symbol.

```
$ LIST == "DIRECTORY/SIZE/DATE/PROTECTION"
```

Just as actual DCL commands may be abbreviated, the symbol may also define abbreviations for the symbol name. The asterisk (*) is used as an abbreviation marker within the symbol name. Hence, the symbol may be specified as either the full command name, the abbreviated name before the abbreviation marker, or any number of characters after the abbreviation marker.

```
$ LI*ST == "DIRECTORY/SIZE/DATE/PROTECTION"
```

Thus, either the full symbol name LIST, the abbreviation LIS or the abbreviation LI may be used to indicate the symbol.

Similar to logical names, symbols definitions are lost when a process terminates and are thus candidates for definition within the LOGIN.COM file executed during process start up. Be sure to define global symbols (using the double equal sign) within the LOGIN.COM file.

When selecting a symbol name, the user may select the same name as an actual DCL verb. By so doing, the DCL verb no longer will invoke the standard function but will perform the new command sentence indicated.

```
$ TYPE == "TYPE/PAGE"
```

Hence, the TYPE command will no longer be interpreted by DCL as the standard TYPE verb, but is rather a symbolic command which is equated by the user to be TYPE/PAGE. Care should be taken not to use actual DCL verb names as the name of symbols, as this will override the DCL verb, unless that is the specific intention.

Extensive use of symbols could actually enhance the DCL environment enough so as to simulate the command language of another environment to a large extent. For example, suppose that we wanted to emulate certain directory maintenance commands provided with the DOS operating system for PCs. We could define the CHANGE DIRECTORY (CD) and MAKE DIRECTORY (MD) commands as DCL symbols, as follows. Thus, from DCL, the user could essentially enter DOS commands.

```
$ CD == "SET DEFAULT"
$ MD == "CREATE/DIRECTORY"

$ CD [SMITH]
$ MD [SMITH.FILES]
```

In the above example, although we have emulated the DOS commands with DCL symbols, the syntax for directory specifications within the parameter must still follow the conventions for DCL and VMS.

We could, however, combine both symbols and logical names within the same command sentence. For example, we could use the LIST symbol as a symbol in place of the DCL verb, and we could use the ACCOUNT logical name as an alias for the physical directory specification. Therefore, the result of the command sentence LIST ACCOUNT is as follows:

```
$ LIST ACCOUNT

Directory EARTH::DUA0:[SMITH.MEMOS.JAN]

FILE1.MEMO;2               1  31-AUG-1989 10:27  (RWED,RWED,RE,R)
FILE1.MEMO;1              9  30-AUG-1989 09:23  (RWED,RWED,RE,R)
FILE2.MEMO;1              1  30-AUG-1989 09:23  (RWED,RWED,RE,R)
FILE3.MEMO;1              1  30-AUG-1989 09:24  (RWED,RWED,RE,R)
```

Symbol Maintenance

The current definition of a symbol may be displayed with the SHOW SYMBOL command.

```
$ SHOW SYMBOL LIST
  LIST = "DIRECTORY/SIZE/DATE/PROTECTION"
```

All symbol definitions may be displayed by including the /ALL qualifier.

```
$ SHOW SYMBOL/ALL
```

All symbol maintenance commands assume that the user is referring to local symbols rather than global symbols. Thus, if we wished to perform the above functions for symbols that were defined as global symbols, we would need to include the /GLOBAL qualifier.

```
$ SHOW SYMBOL/GLOBAL LIST
$ SHOW SYMBOL/GLOBAL/ALL
```

Similar to the change in the definition of a logical name, the definition of a symbol may be overridden simply by using the same symbol name in a new define operation. The following example overrides the definition of the global symbol LIST.

```
$ LIST == "DIRECTORY/SIZE/DATE/PROTECTION"

$ LIST == "DIRECTORY/FULL"
```

As with logical names, symbols are automatically deleted when the user logs off and the process terminates. Within an interactive session though, one or all symbols from either the local or global table may be specifically deleted.

```
$ DELETE/SYMBOL LIST
$ DELETE/SYMBOL/GLOBAL LIST

$ DELETE/SYMBOL/ALL
$ DELETE/SYMBOL/GLOBAL/ALL
```

Chapter 6 Exercises

Within the exercises for this chapter we will define, use and maintain both logical names as an alias for the physical file specification, and symbols as an alias for the DCL verb and associated qualifiers.

Exercise 1
Logical Names

a) Use the DEFINE command to define a logical name called ACCOUNT for a particular subdirectory. Be certain to include the physical subdirectory name within quotes and to follow the standard rules for physical directory names.

b) Enter the following commands to use the logical name. (Substitute an actual file name within your subdirectory for "x").

```
$ DIRECTORY ACCOUNT

$ TYPE ACCOUNT:x
```

c) Use the SHOW LOGICAL command to list the logical names defined.

d) Use the DEFINE command again to change the physical definition of the logical name ACCOUNT to another subdirectory. Use the logical name ACCOUNT within command sentences to now refer to the new subdirectory.

e) Delete the logical name ACCOUNT.

Exercise 2
Symbols

a) Define the global symbol LIST as an equivalent to the command DIRECTORY/SIZE/DATE. Be certain to use the double equal sign to indicate a global symbol.

b) Use the symbol LIST to receive a directory listing of the current default directory. Use the symbol together with a physical directory specification and also the logical name ACCOUNT to receive a directory listing of other subdirectories.

c) Show the definition of the symbol LIST. Be certain to include the qualifier /GLOBAL as the symbol was defined with the double equal sign.

d) Change the definition of the symbol LIST by equating it to the command DIRECTORY/FULL. Use the command LIST once again and observe the change.

e) Delete the symbol LIST. Again, be sure to use the /GLOBAL qualifier on the DELETE/SYMBOL command.

Exercise Answers

Exercise 1a

```
$ DEFINE ACCOUNT "[SMITH.MEMOS.JAN]"
```

Exercise 1b

```
$ DIRECTORY ACCOUNT
$ TYPE ACCOUNT:DAY1.MEMO
```

Exercise 1c

```
$ SHOW LOGICAL ACCOUNT
$ SHOW LOGICAL/TABLE=LNM$PROCESS
```

Exercise 1d

```
$ DEFINE ACCOUNT "[SMITH.MEMOS.FEB]"
$ DIRECTORY ACCOUNT
```

Exercise 1e

```
$ DEASSIGN ACCOUNT
```

Exercise 2a

```
$ LIST == "DIRECTORY/SIZE/DATE"
```

Exercise 2b

```
$ LIST

$ DEFINE ACCOUNT "[SMITH.MEMOS.JAN]"
$ LIST [SMITH.MEMOS.JAN]
$ LIST ACCOUNT
```

Exercise 2c

```
$ SHOW SYMBOL/GLOBAL LIST
```

Exercise 2d

```
$ LIST == "DIRECTORY/FULL"
$ LIST
```

Exercise 2e

```
$ DELETE/SYMBOL/GLOBAL LIST
```

Chapter Seven

Print and Batch Queues

Overview

Queues are created by the system manager to sequentially service requests from users on the system. There are two general classes of queues: print queues and batch queues.

Print queues are established for each print device. Users who wish to use the device to print text files can submit their document or job to the corresponding print queue, which in turn will print the document when all prior jobs have been processed.

Batch queues execute command procedures in batch or background mode, without attachment to a specific terminal for display of the output of the procedure. Thus, a user may have one or more batch jobs running in background mode while simultaneously executing an interactive process from their terminal.

There may be one or more batch queues created for a system and shared by various users. Users may submit their command procedure as a job to one of the batch queues, which will execute their job as a background process when intervening jobs within that batch queue have been processed.

All print jobs and batch jobs submitted by users to the appropriate queues are automatically assigned a sequential entry number by VMS. The entry number is used to identify a job within one of the queues.

There may be several different queues on a particular system, any of which could successfully execute a job. For example, there may be several similar print devices attached to your system, with any one of the devices being equally capable of printing your document. While you may have little preference as to which of the identical devices is used to print your document, it would be convenient if you used the queue which currently had the least amount of printing already queued.

You could manually examine each of the queues and attempt to determine this for yourself or utilize special generic queues that can perform this search automatically. Jobs submitted to a generic queue will search several and perhaps all print devices on your system and automatically select the queue for the print device most likely to process your document first. Thus, if all users select generic queues for printing, the system will automatically balance the load across available printers.

Generic queues may also be established for batch jobs as well. By submitting command procedures to the generic queues, the system will automatically balance the load among all available batch queues.

The queue name SYS$PRINT is generally used by the system manager as the generic print queue for the system. The queue name SYS$BATCH is generally used as the generic batch queue for the system.

The sections that follow describe in detail the submission and control of print and batch jobs within the queues. We will consider the following topics:

- Print jobs
- Batch jobs
- SUBMIT command
- SHOW QUEUE command
- SHOW ENTRY command
- DELETE/ENTRY command
- SET ENTRY command

Print Jobs

The PRINT command submits the files specified to the generic print queue SYS$PRINT. While this queue may have been associated with a specific print device by the system manager, it is likely a generic queue for the system as discussed above.

The following command submits the file FILE1.MEMO for printing.

```
$ PRINT FILE1.MEMO
Job FILE1 (queue SYS$PRINT, entry 363) pending
```

The following rules exist for the PRINT command:

- The queue SYS$PRINT is selected as the default.

- An entry number is assigned the job based upon the next sequential entry number available from the system.

- An alphabetic job name is assigned the job, based upon the file name of the document being printed. This may be overridden with the /NAME qualifier.

- The system informs the user of the job name assigned, the queue selected, the entry number assigned, and whether the job has started processing immediately or is pending. This default message may be refused with the /NOIDENTIFY qualifier.

- The file name extension of .LIS is assumed by the PRINT command if none is given with the file name specification.

- A parameter list and wildcards may be used to select multiple files for printing.

- The following generic qualifiers, discussed earlier, are applicable to the PRINT command as well:

  - /CREATED, /MODIFIED, /EXPIRED, and /BACKUP to be used in conjunction with /BEFORE and /SINCE, selecting files before or since the date indicated.

  - /CONFIRM to prompt the user for a confirmation that the files indicated should actually be printed.

  - /EXCLUDE to specify certain individual files that should be excluded from the files otherwise selected with the command.

Only one copy of the files is printed. Multiple copies of the files may be requested. The following examples request (1) multiple copies of all files for the entire print job and (2) multiple copies of only one file within the print job.

```
$ PRINT -
/COPIES=5 FILE1.MEMO, FILE2.MEMO, FILE3.MEMO

$ PRINT FILE1.MEMO/COPIES=5, -
FILE2.MEMO, FILE3.MEMO
```

Depending upon how the generic queues have been set up by the system manager of your system as well as other factors, you may wish to schedule your job within a specific queue, rather than the generic SYS$PRINT. The following qualifier selects a specific queue for a print job.

```
$ PRINT/QUEUE=PRINTER5 FILE1.MEMO
```

By default, print jobs will begin execution as soon as the queue in which they were submitted has processed all intervening or prior jobs. The /AFTER qualifier permits scheduling of the job for printing after a certain date, after a certain time of today's date, or after a certain date and time in the future. The following illustrates these three options.

```
$ PRINT/AFTER=01-JAN-1990 FILE1.MEMO

$ PRINT/AFTER=13:30 FILE1.MEMO

$ PRINT/AFTER=01-JAN-1990:13:30 FILE1.MEMO
```

A job may be submitted to a queue and held indefinitely. Jobs placed on hold will not execute until specifically released by either the user or system manager or operator (discussed later). The following command submits a file for printing but schedules the job to be held indefinitely.

```
$ PRINT/HOLD FILE1.MEMO
```

There are several qualifiers available for printing informational pages with your job in addition to the document itself. These informational pages help to identify your document from many others which are likely being processed by the same printer. These qualifiers are as follows:

- **/HEADER** for a header line. A one-line heading message including the file name and user name is printing on the top line of each page within your document.

- **/FLAG** for a flag page. A supplemental page is printed just before the first page of your document, listing in large print the file name, user name and other characteristics of the job.

- **/TRAILER** for a trailer page. A supplemental page, similar to the flag page, is printed after the last page of your document and before the first page of the next user's print job.

- **/BURST** for a burst page. A supplemental page printed at the end of your document, similar to the trailer page, that includes a pattern of characters that prints over the perforation between the trailer page of your document and the flag page of the next user's document. Such a pattern permits the printer operator to quickly thumb through a stack of printer output and separate the jobs.

The following examples illustrate the use of these options. Several qualifiers may be included within the same command for a series of additional informational pages to be added to the print out in addition to the actual file data.

```
$ PRINT/HEADER FILE1.MEMO

$ PRINT/FLAG FILE1.MEMO

$ PRINT/TRAILER FILE1.MEMO

$ PRINT/BURST FILE1.MEMO

$ PRINT/HEADER/FLAG/TRAILER/BURST FILE1.MEMO
```

Finally, you may request that a notification message be sent to your terminal once the print job has completed. Any interactive user who is logged in with your user name at the time the print job is completed will receive this message. This is requested as follows:

```
$ PRINT/NOTIFY FILE1.MEMO
```

Batch Jobs

Very similar to print jobs, batch jobs are submitted to either a generic queue or a specific execution queue for processing. The main difference, of course, is that while files submitted as print jobs are documents to be printed, files submitted as batch jobs are command procedures to be executed in background mode.

Once a batch job becomes the current entry within the batch queue, the following activities take place:

- A background process is created for the job.

- The background process logs in using the same user name as the user who submitted the job.

- As part of the login for the background process, the batch job executes the LOGIN.COM and other start-up procedures just like an interactive process would during its login activity.

- All output for the batch job is sent to a log file.

The log file is most important to the user in determining the result of the batch job. Since the job executes in background mode without attachment to any terminal, the only way that the user may determine the result of the job, including any possible errors, is to examine the output recorded in the log file.

By default, log files are created and processed as follows. This default processing may be overridden, as we will see later in this section.

• The log file is assigned the same name as the command procedure executing, with an extension of .LOG.

• The log file is created within the main directory level of the account, regardless of which directory the command procedure is stored in.

• Once the batch process has completed, the log file is automatically submitted to the generic print queue SYS$PRINT for printing.

• The log file is deleted once it has been printed from the print queue SYS$PRINT.

SUBMIT

The SUBMIT command submits the command procedure files specified to the generic batch queue SYS$BATCH. While this queue may have been associated with a specific batch queue by the system manager, it is likely a generic batch queue that searches other execution batch queues on the system, similar to the generic print queue SYS$PRINT.

A command procedure is submitted as a batch job with the following command:

```
$ SUBMIT PROCEDURE1.COM
Job PROCEDURE1 (queue SYS$BATCH, entry 364) started on SYS$BATCH
```

The following rules exist for the SUBMIT command and are very similar to those for PRINT:

• The queue SYS$BATCH is selected as the default.

• An entry number is assigned the job based upon the next sequential entry number available from the system.

- An alphabetic job name is assigned the job, based upon the file name of the command procedure being submitted. This may be overridden with the /NAME qualifier.

- The system informs the user of the job name assigned, the queue selected, the entry number assigned, and whether the job has started processing immediately or is pending. This default message may be refused with the /NOIDENTIFY qualifier.

- The file name extension of .COM is assumed by the SUBMIT command if none is given with the file name specification.

- A parameter list and wildcards may be used to select multiple files for execution.

- The following generic qualifiers, discussed earlier, are applicable to the SUBMIT command as well:

    - /CREATED, /MODIFIED, /EXPIRED, and /BACKUP to be used in conjunction with /BEFORE and /SINCE, selecting files before or since the date indicated.

    - /CONFIRM to prompt the user for a confirmation that the files indicated should actually be submitted.

    - /EXCLUDE to specify certain individual files which should be excluded from the files otherwise selected with the command.

The following qualifiers are permitted for the batch jobs and the SUBMIT command identically as for the PRINT command.

- **/QUEUE** selects a specific batch queue other than the default SYS$BATCH.

- **/AFTER** schedules a job for execution after a certain time today, after a certain date, and after a certain future date and time.

- **/HOLD** holds a job indefinitely within the queue, until released by the user or an operator or system manager.

- **/NOTIFY** notifies the user with a terminal message that the batch job has completed execution and the log file may be examined to determine the result.

As mentioned, by default the log file is created in the user's initial default directory (usually the top-level directory) and assigned the same name as the command procedure with an extension of .LOG. This may be overridden with the /LOG_FILE qualifier of the SUBMIT command.

The first example causes the log file to be created within a specific subdirectory. The second example assigns a specific file name to the log file. The third example overrides both the placement and the naming of the log file.

```
$ SUBMIT/LOG_FILE=[SMITH.BATCH] BATCH1.COM

$ SUBMIT/LOG_FILE=RUN22.LOG BATCH1.COM

$ SUBMIT -
/LOG_FILE=[SMITH.BATCH]RUN22.LOG BATCH1.COM
```

Additionally, the log file, regardless of its name or location, will automatically be submitted to the print queue SYS$PRINT for printing and deleted once it has been successfully printed. These defaults may also be overridden using the qualifiers listed:

- **/PRINTER** selects a print queue other than SYS$PRINT for printing of the log file.

- **/KEEP** requests that the log file remain or be kept on the disk even after printing

- **/NOPRINT** requests that the batch log not be submitted to any print queue and be kept on the disk for examination by the user.

The following examples illustrate these options.

```
$ SUBMIT/PRINTER=PRINTER5 BATCH1.COM

$ SUBMIT/KEEP BATCH1.COM

$ SUBMIT/NOPRINT BATCH1.COM
```

SHOW QUEUE

Our discussion for batch and print queues thus far has assumed that the user wishes to use either the default generic queues or is aware of the names of alternate execution queues. The following command lists all queues on the system, both print and batch queues, as well as generic and execution queues. Any pending or executing entries that the user has within the queues are also displayed.

```
$ SHOW QUEUE
```

Alternately, the user may list a specific queue, which will also display any pending jobs for the user. Assume that the user SIDERIS submits the batch job BATCH1.COM to the queue SYS$BATCH.

```
$ SUBMIT/QUEUE=SYS$BATCH/AFTER=01-JAN-1990 BATCH1.COM
Job BATCH1 (queue _SI860B_BATCH, entry 451) holding until  1-JAN-1990 00:00
$
```

We could then examine the queues and the entry number 451 within the queue with either the SHOW QUEUE command (for all queues) or the SHOW QUEUE SYS$BATCH command (to list only that queue).

```
$ SHOW QUEUE SYS$BATCH
Batch queue _SI860B_BATCH, on SI860B::

  Jobname      Username     Entry      Status
  -------      --------     -----      ------
  BATCH1       SIDERIS        451      Holding until   1-JAN-1990 00:00
```

In addition to listing all queues, the user may (1) list all batch queues, (2) list all queues for print devices, and (3) list generic queues only. Note the following examples:

```
$ SHOW QUEUE/BATCH
```

```
$ SHOW QUEUE/DEVICE
```

```
$ SHOW QUEUE/GENERIC
```

Regardless of which queues are listed, only your own print or batch jobs are displayed within the queues. Provided that you have read access to other users' jobs, you may request a display of all users' jobs within the queues, in addition to your own, as shown below.

```
$ SHOW QUEUE/ALL
```

As can be noted, a brief display is provided of the queues and the entries within those queues. A complete or full display regarding the queues and entries may be selected with the /FULL qualifier.

Using both /ALL and /FULL, without naming any specific queue, will create a full display of all users' jobs within all batch and print queues.

```
$  SHOW  QUEUE/FULL

$  SHOW  QUEUE/ALL/FULL
```

The generic /OUTPUT qualifier considered for other commands is applicable with the SHOW QUEUE command also. The output from the command is directed to the text file indicated.

SHOW ENTRY

Rather than using the SHOW QUEUE command to list all the queues on the system, including those in which you have no jobs currently placed, you may select only those queues in which you currently have entries. This may be done with the SHOW ENTRY command.

```
$ SHOW ENTRY
   Jobname          Username      Entry  Blocks  Status
   -------          --------      -----  ------  ------

   BATCH1           SIDERIS        451            Holding until  1-JAN-1990 00:00
     On batch queue _SI860B_BATCH
```

Of all the queues and entries on the system, only your own entries are listed and the queue in which it has been placed displayed.

As with SHOW QUEUE, the /FULL qualifier may be used to generate a full listing of the entry.

```
$ SHOW ENTRY/FULL
  Jobname          Username       Entry  Blocks  Status
  -------          --------       -----  ------  ------

  BATCH1           SIDERIS          451          Holding until  1-JAN-1990 00:00
    On batch queue _SI860B_BATCH
    Submitted  1-SEP-1989 13:43 /PRIORITY=100
    File: _$1$DUS3:[SIDERIS]BATCH1.COM;1
```

Also similar to the SHOW QUEUE command, we may show only those entries that are within the batch queues or the print queues with the following qualifiers.

```
$ SHOW ENTRY/BATCH

$ SHOW ENTRY/DEVICE
```

A specific batch or print entry may be located and the status displayed by naming the entry number.

```
$ SHOW ENTRY 100
```

If you have read access to other users' entries, you may selectively display the entries found within the queues for a specific user name, as follows:

```
$ SHOW ENTRY/USER=JONES
```

The generic /OUTPUT qualifier is permitted for SHOW ENTRY.

DELETE/ENTRY

Batch or print jobs which are currently executing or pending within a queue may be deleted by naming the entry number. You must have delete access to another user's entries in order for you to delete entries that are not owned by your process.

Entries are deleted with the DELETE/ENTRY command.

```
$ DELETE/ENTRY=100
```

Multiple entries may be deleted with a single command.

```
$ DELETE/ENTRY=(100,101,102)
```

In each of these examples the entries specified are deleted from whatever queues they are found in. You may specifically name a queue, in addition to the entry number, as an extra check to ensure that the entry is deleted only if found within the queue specified.

```
$ DELETE/ENTRY=100 SYS$BATCH
```

SET ENTRY

We have just considered the DELETE/ENTRY command which deletes an entry from a queue. While you may not wish to delete an entry, there may be certain characteristics of a job that you wish to change from what was specified when the job was first scheduled. The SET ENTRY command permits the job characteristics of either print or batch jobs to be modified as they are pending within the queue.

Earlier we discussed the /HOLD qualifier for both the PRINT and SUBMIT commands, which schedules a print or batch job to be held indefinitely until specifically released. Such a release of a job that is being held is done by naming the entry with the SET ENTRY/NOHOLD command as follows:

```
$ SET ENTRY 100/NOHOLD
```

Conversely, an entry that is scheduled to execute immediately, as soon as the entry becomes the current one within the queue, may be held as follows.

```
$ SET ENTRY 100/HOLD
```

If a job is pending until a certain date and time, as a result of the /AFTER qualifier, we may release the job immediately by means of the /RELEASE qualifier.

The /RELEASE qualifier can also be used to release a job that is held, similar to /NOHOLD. However, /NOHOLD will not release a job that was scheduled for a specific date or time with the /AFTER qualifier. This can only be done with /RELEASE.

```
$ SET ENTRY 100/RELEASE
```

Rather than releasing an entry for immediate execution, you may wish to alter the scheduled time, as shown in the next example. If the new time selected has already passed, it has the same effect as /RELEASE and makes the entry available for immediate execution.

```
$ SET ENTRY 100/AFTER=14:00
```

Notice the example below where the batch job BATCH1.COM, submitted in an earlier example but scheduled for execution immediately past midnight of the first of January in 1990, has been changed with the SET ENTRY command.

```
$ SET ENTRY 451/AFTER=01-FEB-1990:10:00
$ SHOW ENTRY 451
  Jobname          Username        Entry  Blocks  Status
  --------         --------        -----  ------  ------
  BATCH1           SIDERIS          451           Holding until  1-FEB-1990 10:00
    On batch queue _SI860B_BATCH
```

The /NOTIFY option may be either added or removed from a pending entry as follows:

```
$ SET ENTRY 100/NOTIFY
```

```
$ SET ENTRY 100/NONOTIFY
```

For print jobs, any of the qualifiers that may have been selected when the job was scheduled with the PRINT command may be now modified with the SET ENTRY command.

```
$ SET ENTRY 100/NOFLAG/NOTRAILER
```

Likewise, any of the qualifiers used with the SUBMIT command may be altered.

```
$ SET ENTRY 100/NOKEEP/PRINT=PRINTER5
```

Chapter 7 Exercises

Within the exercises for this chapter we will do the following:

- Examine all print and batch queues on the system;
- Schedule a print job for printing;
- Schedule a batch job for execution;
- Examine all print and batch entries we have submitted on the system;
- Delete an entry that has been scheduled;
- Modify certain characteristics for an entry that has been scheduled.

Exercise 1
Print Jobs

a) Use the SHOW QUEUE/DEVICE command to view the print queues on your system and select a print queue to be used.

b) Schedule a document file as a print job for printing late tonight with the command PRINT/AFTER=23:00.

c) Use both the SHOW QUEUE and SHOW ENTRY commands to view the print job just scheduled.

d) Schedule another print job using some of the qualifiers considered, such as /FLAG, /HEADER, /TRAILER, etc.

Exercise 2
Batch Jobs

Before attempting to schedule a batch job, first create a sample command procedure as follows:

```
$ CREATE SAMPLE.COM
$ SHOW USERS
$ SHOW TIME
$ SHOW SYSTEM
^ Z
```

Next, execute the command procedure interactively so that you may view the correct output from the procedure.

```
$  @SAMPLE.COM
```

With this sample procedure, you now have a file that you may submit as a batch job and use within the exercise.

a) Use the SHOW QUEUE/BATCH command to view the batch queues on your system and select a batch queue to be used.

b) Schedule a command procedure for execution late tonight with the SUBMIT/AFTER=23:00 command.

c) Use both the SHOW QUEUE and SHOW ENTRY commands to view the batch job just scheduled.

d) Schedule another batch job for immediate execution using the qualifier /KEEP to keep the resulting log file stored on the disk and the /NOTIFY qualifier to inform you of when the job completes.

e) Use the TYPE command to examine the log file once the batch job has completed.

Exercise 3
Maintenance of Entries

a) Use the SHOW ENTRY command to examine all print and batch entries currently scheduled.

b) Select an entry number for deletion and use the DELETE/ENTRY command to delete the job. Use SHOW ENTRY or SHOW QUEUE again to confirm that the entry has been deleted.

c) Select another entry number for modification. Use the SET ENTRY command along with appropriate qualifiers for print and batch jobs to change the attributes of the entry. Use SHOW ENTRY or SHOW QUEUE again to confirm that the entry has been modified.

Depending upon the qualifier you have altered, you may have to include the /FULL qualifier with the SHOW ENTRY or SHOW

QUEUE commands in order to see the effect of the change you have made.

Exercise Answers

These answers assume that the print queue selected is SAMPLE$PRINT, that the batch queue selected is SAMPLE$BATCH and that the entry number of all jobs is 100. Within your actual entry of the commands, substitute SAMPLE$PRINT with the name of the print queue that you have selected, substitute SAMPLE$BATCH with the name of the batch queue that you have selected, and substitute entry 100 with the actual entry numbers assigned the jobs.

Exercise 1a

Self-explanatory

Exercise 1b

```
$ PRINT/AFTER=23:00/QUEUE=SAMPLE$PRINT DAY1.MEMO
```

Exercise 1c

```
$ SHOW ENTRY
$ SHOW QUEUE
```

Exercise 1d

```
$PRINT/AFTER=22:00 -
/FLAG/HEADER/TRAILER/QUEUE=SAMPLE$PRINT DAY2.MEMO
```

Exercise 2a

Self-explanatory

Exercise 2b

```
$ SUBMIT/AFTER=23:00/QUEUE=SAMPLE$BATCH SAMPLE.COM
```

Exercise 2c

```
$  SHOW  QUEUE
$  SHOW  ENTRY
```

Exercise 2d

```
$  SUBMIT/KEEP/NOTIFY/QUEUE=SAMPLE$BATCH  SAMPLE.COM
```

Exercise 2e

```
$  TYPE  SYS$LOGIN:SAMPLE.COM
```

Exercise 3a

Self-explanatory

Exercise 3b

```
$  DELETE/ENTRY=100
$  SHOW  QUEUE
$  SHOW  ENTRY
```

Exercise 3c

```
$  SHOW  ENTRY
$  SET  ENTRY  100  -
/NOFLAG/NOHEADER/NOTRAILER/AFTER=19:00

$  SHOW  QUEUE/FULL
$  SHOW  ENTRY/FULL
```

Chapter Eight

EVE Editor

Overview

The VMS operating system provides two standard text editors for users to create and modify text files, namely, the Extensible VAX Editor (EVE) and EDT. Both are full-screen, interactive editors and both are very popular among VAX users.

The EDT editor is probably the more commonly used editor among long-time VAX users, due largely to the fact that it is the original editor for the VMS operating system and the one most familiar to such users. However, those with experience in both editors, including long-time and newer users, generally agree that the EVE editor is both more powerful and comprehensive, while at the same time being easier to use than EDT.

EDT's most popular feature is the functional numeric keypad, where a single key on the numeric keypad of the terminal is redefined to an editor function and can invoke the entire function or operation by the user pressing the single key. While this feature is not available within EVE itself, the version of EVE available with VMS version 5.0 or later includes an emulation mode where the entire EDT keypad is active within the EVE editor.

Considering ease of use and the superior functionality of EVE over EDT, together with the fact that EVE can now emulate EDT's most important feature, the functional numeric keypad, our discussion of an editor within this textbook will consider the EVE editor and its EDT emulation. The appendix, however, contains some limited information regarding EDT for those who are interested.

EVE Overview

The EVE editor is based upon the Text Processing Utility (TPU) of VMS. TPU is used not only as the basis for EVE, but also for other editors such as the Language Sensitive Editor (LSE) and other user-developed editors.

One of the reasons that EVE, despite its extensive functionality, is so easy to use is the amount of on-line help available. Within this section we will consider

134

the following help modes that are available on-line when working within an EVE session:

- Help on the EVE function keys
- Help on EVE's emulation of the EDT keypad
- Help for EVE command mode

The editor is invoked by specifying the /TPU qualifier of the EDIT command. You may wish to define a symbol discussed earlier to invoke the editor as well. Note the following examples:

```
$ EDIT/TPU FILE1.MEMO

        or

$ EVE == "EDIT/TPU"
$ EVE FILE1.MEMO
```

The following rules apply when specifying a file name with the EDIT/TPU command.

- Naming a non-existent file will create a blank EVE buffer in which the user may enter the text for the new file. The EVE buffer is assigned the same name as the file. When the session is terminated, the contents of the buffer are written to disk and the first version of the file is created.

- Naming an existing file that was already created will load the contents of the file into an EVE buffer of the same name and allow user modification of the data. Once the editing session is complete, a new version of the file will be created and the modified data written to the file.

- Failing to name any file will provide the user with an empty EVE buffer named MAIN. The user may enter any text desired within this buffer. Once the editing session is complete, the user will be prompted for a required file name in which the data will be stored. If the file name given is already in existence, a new version will be created.

Once the EVE session has been invoked and one of the above described buffers is displayed, the user may enter any text from the keyboard. The user may delete a character by using the DELETE key located just above the RETURN key. To terminate an EVE session and save the contents of the session to a disk file, the user must press the CONTROL Z key.

EVE has a very flexible and powerful command level, which will be considered later within this chapter. An EVE command is entered as follows:

- Press the DO function key to receive the EVE command prompt
- Enter the EVE command
- Press the RETURN or DO keys to terminate the command

In the following example, we invoke the editor with the EDIT/TPU command and name a new file called FILE1.MEMO. A blank EVE buffer also named FILE1.MEMO is created and the user may enter text. At the bottom of the screen is the EVE status line. Also notice the command prompt that is displayed when the DO key is pressed to enter the EVE command level.

```
Buffer: FILE1.MEMO                               | Write | Insert | Forward
Command:
```

The EVE status line displays the following information:

- The name of the current buffer is displayed on the screen and available to the user.

- Whether the buffer is a WRITE or READ ONLY buffer, that is, whether or not the user may modify text within the buffer. By default, user buffers are WRITE buffers which can be modified.

- Whether the current editing mode is INSERT or OVERSTRIKE. By default, user buffers are initially in INSERT mode.

- Whether the EVE direction is currently set to FORWARD or REVERSE. The EVE direction affects several commands that we will consider. By default, user buffers are initially set to a FORWARD direction.

EVE Editing Keypad

The editing keys that are available for EVE include (1) the arrow keys and (2) the editing keypad.

There are four arrow keys available, UP, DOWN, LEFT and RIGHT, each of which performs a separate function to move the cursor within the buffer. These keys may also be combined with the EDT GOLD key, discussed later, to perform other functions. These functions are as follows:

- LEFT, move one character to the left
- GOLD LEFT, move to the beginning of the line

- RIGHT, move one character to the right
- GOLD RIGHT, move to the end of the line

- DOWN, move one line down
- GOLD DOWN, move to the bottom of the document

- UP, move one line up
- GOLD UP, move to the top of the document

Users with DEC terminal models VT200 or later, or clones of those models, include an editing keypad. The editing keypad is located just above the arrow keys. Their function is similar, although not identical, for both EVE and EDT. We will now consider their function within the context of EVE. Notice the keypad diagram below for these keys.

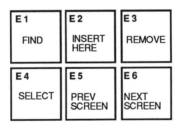

FIND

The FIND function prompts the user for a string of characters. The user must enter the characters to search for, terminated by either the RETURN or DO keys. EVE begins the search at the current cursor position and changes the position to the beginning of the next occurrence of the search text, if found.

If the search text is not found, a message is displayed and the current cursor position is unchanged.

Whether the current EVE direction is forward or reverse, as indicated by the EVE status display line, will determine in which direction EVE attempts to find the next occurrence of the text.

If EVE cannot find an occurrence of the text using the current direction but can locate the text in the opposite direction, the user will be given the option to search in the opposite direction. Note the following example requiring a user response of either Y or N:

```
Buffer: FILE1.MEMO .                          | Write | Insert | Forward
Found in reverse direction. Go there?
```

The user may find the next occurrence of the search text most recently entered by simply pressing the FIND key twice (double FIND).

PREV SCREEN
The PREVIOUS SCREEN key moves the cursor position forward 16 lines. If there are less than 16 additional lines within the document, the cursor is positioned at the bottom of the text file.

NEXT SCREEN
The NEXT SCREEN key moves the cursor position backwards 16 lines. If there are fewer than 16 lines prior to the current cursor position, the cursor is positioned at the top of the text file.

SELECT
The SELECT key is used to mark the current cursor position as the beginning of a region of text that will be selected for special processing, such as a "cut" or "remove" function.

After pressing the SELECT key, the user must then use one of the cursor positioning features of EVE, such as NEXT, PREVIOUS SCREEN, one of the ARROW keys, etc. As the cursor moves, the text region selected is highlighted in reverse video beginning from the selected point to the present cursor position.

In the example that follows, the user wishes to select and highlight the second line of text, to be included within a "cut" and "paste" operation. The user must move to the beginning of the second line of text. At that current cursor position, the second line of text may be selected by pressing the SELECT key to mark the selection point and pressing the DOWN arrow key to move the cursor one line down, thereby highlighting the second line of text.

The user may UNSELECT the highlighted text by pressing the SELECT key again before performing any operation on the text.

```
This is line one.
This is line two.
This is line three.
```

REMOVE

Once the user has selected and highlighted a region of text, the REMOVE key allows the user to remove or "cut" the text out from the buffer. The text is stored in the "remove buffer" and may be used as part of a "paste" or "insert" operation later.

Note the result of pressing the REMOVE key while the second line of text is selected and highlighted.

```
This is line one.
This is line three.
```

INSERT HERE

The INSERT HERE key inserts the text currently stored within the "remove buffer" into the buffer. The location of the insertion is at the current cursor position.

Note in the final step of the cut and paste operation where the user employs the cursor positioning keys to move the cursor to the end of the text and presses INSERT HERE. The line of text that was originally located at line two has been "cut" and inserted at the end of line three.

```
This is line one.
This is line three.
This is line two.
```

A typical "cut and paste" function would therefore require the following steps.

- Position the cursor to the beginning of the text to be removed and press SELECT.

- Use any cursor positioning key to move the cursor forward or back, highlighting the text as the cursor is moved.

- Once the text area to be removed is highlighted, press the REMOVE key to "cut" the text.

- Use the cursor positioning features of EVE to position the cursor to the location of the insertion and press the INSERT HERE key.

EVE Function Keys

In addition to the editing keypad and the arrow keys, EVE does make limited use of the keyboard function keys, although not to the extent of EDT. The EVE function keys used by EVE are located at the top of the keyboard and are as follows:

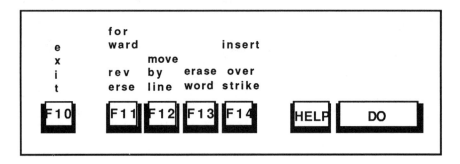

DO
Invokes (and also terminates) EVE command mode. Valid EVE commands that may be entered in command mode are considered throughout the latter sections within this chapter.

HELP
Displays a diagram of the EVE function keys shown above and the EDT functional keypad.

F10
EXIT function to terminate the EVE session and create a new version of the file. Identical to CONTROL Z or the EXIT command.

F11
FORWARD/REVERSE. Toggles the current EVE direction between forward and reverse. The current EVE direction is displayed on the EVE status line and is altered as the F11 key is pressed.

Various EVE functions, such as FIND and others, use the current EVE direction when performing the function.

The initial default is forward.

F12
MOVE BY LINE. A cursor positioning key to move the cursor either forward or reverse one line, depending upon the current EVE direction displayed on the status line.

F13
ERASE WORD. Erases the word where the cursor is currently positioned.

F14
INSERT/OVERSTRIKE. Toggles the current EVE editing mode between insert and overstrike. The current EVE editing mode is displayed on the EVE status line and is updated as the F14 key is pressed. The initial default for a new editing session is insert.

EDT Keypad Emulation

The number of EVE functions which are available from a single key are fairly limited and have already been considered. While the command mode of EVE that we will consider later within this chapter is very powerful, it is cumbersome to have to enter an entire command for every function not available with the limited number of EVE function keys.

EVE's emulation of the EDT keypad solves this dilemma, while also providing a familiar interface for long-time EDT users. EVE's emulation of the EDT keypad is shown below.

The PF1 key is defined as the GOLD key within EDT. When the GOLD key is used in combination with a function key, the function key has an alternate meaning. We referred to the GOLD key when describing the ARROW keys. If EDT keypad emulation has been invoked, and the GOLD key is, therefore, available, we may press the GOLD key, followed by one of the arrow keys, to perform a separate function.

With regard to the EDT keypad, each key performs the top function listed on the key cap diagram . When the GOLD key and the EDT function key are pressed, the bottom function listed on the key cap is performed. By using the GOLD key in this way, each of the arrow keys and the EDT function keys can perform two separate functions.

PF1	PF2	PF3	PF4
GOLD	HELP HELP IND	FIND NEXT FIND	DELETE L UNDEL L
7	**8**	**9**	**-**
PAGE COMMAND	SECTION FILL	APPEND REPLACE	DELETE W UNDEL W
4	**5**	**6**	**,**
FORWARD BOTTOM	REVERSE TOP	CUT PASTE	DELETE C UNDEL C
1	**2**	**3**	**ENTER**
WORD CH CASE	END OF L DEL EOL	CHARAC SPEC INS	ENTER
0		**.**	SUBS
NEXT LINE NEW LINE		SELECT RESET	

By default, the EDT keypad is not emulated within EVE when the editing session is first begun. The first command that follows activates EDT emulation. The second example deactivates EDT emulation. (The DO key must first be pressed before entering any commands. The commands must be terminated with either the DO key or the RETURN key.)

```
SET KEYPAD EDT

SET KEYPAD NOEDT
```

EVE's emulation of the EDT keypad is as follows. These keypad functions have been grouped according to the following types of operations:

- Editing Keys
- Cursor Positioning Keys

- Cut and Paste Keys
- Session Control Keys

You will note that most of the functions available from the EDT keypad are also available either from the EVE function keys that we have already considered or from EVE commands that we will consider later within the chapter. Also bear in mind that several of the functions are duplicates of other functions, that is, different ways of performing the same function.

Editing Keys

PF4
ERASE LINE. Erases the line where the cursor is currently positioned.

GOLD PF4
RESTORE LINE. Restores or "pastes" in the current cursor position the line most recently erased with the ERASE LINE function.

- (dash)
ERASE WORD. Erases the word where the cursor is currently positioned.

GOLD -
RESTORE WORD. Restores or "pastes" in the current cursor position the word most recently erased with the ERASE WORD function.

, (comma)
ERASE CHARACTER. Erases the character where the cursor is currently positioned.

GOLD ,
RESTORE CHARACTER. Restores or "pastes" in the current cursor position the character most recently erased with the ERASE CHARACTER function.

GOLD 2
DELETE END OF LINE. Erases to the end of the current line, beginning at the current cursor position.

GOLD 1
CHANGE CASE. Changes the case of the character where the cursor is currently positioned or of all currently highlighted text.

GOLD 0
OPEN LINE. Insert a blank line at the current cursor position.

Cursor Positioning Keys

GOLD PF3
FIND. Enter search text and search for the next occurrence.

PF3
FIND NEXT. Find the next occurrence of the current search text.

7
MOVE BY PAGE. Moves the cursor to the next page break.

8
NEXT/PREVIOUS SCREEN. Moves the cursor forward or reverse one screen section of text, depending upon the current EVE direction.

GOLD 4
BOTTOM. Moves the cursor to the bottom of the document.

GOLD DOWN ARROW
BOTTOM. Moves the cursor to the bottom of the document.

GOLD 5
TOP. Moves the cursor to the top of the document.

GOLD UP ARROW
TOP. Moves the cursor to the top of the document.

GOLD RIGHT ARROW
END OF LINE. Moves the cursor to the end of the current line.

GOLD LEFT ARROW
START OF LINE. Moves the cursor to the beginning of the current line.

1
MOVE BY WORD. Moves the cursor to the next word.

2
END OF LINE. Moves the cursor to the end of the current line.

3
CHARACTER. Moves the cursor to the next character.

0
MOVE BY LINE. Moves the cursor to the next line.

Cut And Paste Keys

. (period)
SELECT. Marks the beginning of a block of text.

GOLD .
RESET. Unselects or removes the mark for the beginning of a text block.

6
REMOVE. Following a select and cursor movement to highlight a block of text, this function removes or "cuts" the text and stores it in the "cut" buffer.

GOLD 6
INSERT HERE. Inserts or "pastes" the text from the "cut" buffer at the current cursor position.

9
APPEND. Following a select and cursor movement to highlight a block of text, this function removes or "cuts" the text and appends the text into the "cut" buffer. Different from REMOVE, which replaces the text in the "cut" buffer, appends adds the highlighted text to what is already stored in the "cut" buffer.

GOLD 9
REPLACE. Following a select and cursor movement to highlight a block of text, this function cuts the text highlighted and replaces it with the current contents of the paste buffer.

GOLD REMOVE
COPY. This function uses the GOLD key from the EDT keypad and the REMOVE key from the editing keypad to invoke the COPY function. This function copies the text highlighted into the "cut buffer" without removing the highlighted text from its original position. The "cut buffer" may then be "pasted" or inserted into a new location.

Session Control Keys

PF2
HELP. Displays help screens for the EVE function keys and EDT keypad emulation. Synonymous with pressing the HELP function key.

GOLD PF2
KEY DEFINITIONS HELP. A display of the control keys active within EVE.

GOLD 7
Enter command mode. The command mode provided is EVE command mode and not EDT command mode.

GOLD 8
FILL. Fills the text currently highlighted according to the current margin settings. (A complete discussion of the EVE FILL command, along with margin settings, is considered within a later section of this chapter.)

ENTER
Terminates the current EVE command entered within command mode.

4
Set EVE direction forward.

5
Set EVE direction reverse.

GOLD 3
SPECIAL INSERT. Allows the entry of special characters that cannot be input using the standard keyboard, such as control characters and other special characters. Special insert operation is as follows:

- Determine the ASCII code of the special character you wish to insert. Press the GOLD key followed by the ASCII decimal code number. (Do not use the function keypad to enter the ASCII decimal number). The decimal number entered is displayed on the bottom left-hand corner of the screen.

- Press GOLD 3 (SPECIAL INSERT). The display equivalent to the decimal ASCII code entered will be inserted into the current cursor position.

To illustrate, if we wish to enter the paragraph symbol (¶) within the text file, we cannot do so by simply entering a key, as there is no key on the standard keyboard for this symbol. However, by determining the ASCII decimal code number for the symbol (which is 182) we can enter the key sequence GOLD 182 GOLD 3. Note the example:

```
We will enter the paragraph symbol, which is ASCII code # 182 ¶
[End of file]
```

Command Mode Overview

While the EVE and EDT keypad functions are convenient and easy to use, the real power of EVE is available from the advanced functions within command mode. Among the many powerful features of EVE command mode are the following operations:

- Modification of several files within the same EVE editing session, by storing the files within separate EVE buffers.

- Display of multiple EVE buffers on the screen simultaneously with EVE "windows".

- Advanced editing and control commands.

- All EVE and EDT keypad functions have corresponding EVE commands that perform the same functions.

It is very helpful to remember the following rules and features regarding EVE command mode.

- EVE commands are entered by pressing the DO function key, entering the EVE command at the bottom of the screen and terminating the command with either the DO function key, the RETURN key or the ENTER key from the EDT keypad.

- On-line help on all EVE commands may be received by entering the HELP command at EVE command level.

- The most recent EVE command entered may be executed again by pressing the DO key twice (double DO).

- Any EVE command or EVE/EDT function key operation may be repeated multiple times by entering the command REPEAT x, followed by the EVE command or the EVE/EDT function key. By prefacing the command or function with the REPEAT command, the next function will be repeated that number of times.

- All EVE commands may be abbreviated when entered to as few characters as would make the command unique among other EVE commands. If too few characters are entered to distinguish the command from others, a temporary window is created on the screen and the user is shown all EVE commands that begin with the characters entered. The desired command may then be selected.

  Note the following example. The user ambiguously enters the command ERAS, which could indicate ERASE LINE, ERASE CHARACTER and so on. EVE displays a special window showing all the possible commands that begin with the characters ERAS, and the user may complete the command.

```
┌──────────────────────────────────────────────────────────────────┐
│ Erase start of line      Erase previous word       Erase word      │
│ Erase line               Erase character                           │
│                                                                    │
│                                                                    │
│ ▌Choices                                                          ▐│
│ Command: ERAS                                                      │
│ Ambiguous command name: ERAS                                      │
└──────────────────────────────────────────────────────────────────┘
```

As we have already considered, the editing session may be terminated (the EXIT function) by pressing either the CONTROL Z key or EVE function key 10 (F10). The session may also be terminated from command level as follows:

- Entering the EXIT command. This is identical to CONTROL Z and F10.

- Entering the QUIT command. This also ends the editing session, but will not save the results of the editing session. The file remains unchanged.

With this background information regarding EVE command mode in mind, we will now consider the following functions available with EVE commands entered following the DO key:

- Cursor movement
- Basic editing features
- Cut and Paste
- Text alignment
- Text display
- Buffers
- Windows
- Initialization and Command files
- Advanced functions

Cursor Movement

Cursor movement is first determined by the current "cursor mode" within EVE. A "bound" cursor is one that can be positioned only where text has already been entered. To move a "bound" cursor to an area where some text or spaces have not already been entered, the user must insert spaces or blank lines first. A "free" cursor can move anywhere within the display screen, regardless of whether there is text, blank lines, or nothing at all. If the user moves a "free" cursor to a point within the screen display where there is no text and enters a character, the necessary spaces and blank lines are automatically inserted.

Also remember that cursor movement is always affected by the current EVE direction, either forward or reverse.

The cursor mode may be set as follows. By default, the cursor is "free":

```
SET  CURSOR  BOUND

SET  CURSOR  FREE
```

Equivalents of the TOP and BOTTOM functions within EDT keypad emulation are also available at EVE command level. Additional cursor movement functions previously discussed may be performed by means of EVE commands as well.

```
T O P

BOTTOM

MOVE  BY  WORD

MOVE  BY  LINE
```

Within the section on EDT keypad emulation we considered the MOVE BY PAGE function, which moves the cursor to the next page break within the document. Page breaks are not automatically inserted by EVE, however. The following command inserts a page break at the current cursor position. The MOVE BY PAGE function may then be performed by using the EDT keypad function or entering the command equivalent, as follows:

```
INSERT  PAGE

MOVE  BY  PAGE
```

The EVE command equivalent for entering search text and finding the first occurrence of the text is as follows. The example searches for the first occurrence of the word "problem."

```
FIND  problem
```

Basic Editing Features

Most of the basic editing features provided by the EDT and EVE function keys are duplicated within command mode. Note the following EVE commands that duplicate the basic editing features already discussed with EDT or EVE function keys:

```
ERASE  CHARACTER

ERASE  WORD

ERASE  LINE
```

You will recall that the EDT function keys also provided for restoring or "undeleting" the most recent character, word or line deleted. Again, command mode equivalents are provided as follows. Simply entering the RESTORE command will restore whatever was most recently erased.

```
RESTORE  CHARACTER

RESTORE  WORD

RESTORE  LINE

RESTORE
```

In addition to the above, the following ERASE commands, for which there are no function key equivalents, allow erasure of the previous word or erasure of all text from the current cursor position to the start of the line.

```
ERASE  PREVIOUS  WORD

ERASE  START  OF  LINE
```

The case (either uppercase or lowercase) of a word may be changed within command mode. The commands that follow alter the case of the current word (as indicated by the cursor position) or the area of text currently highlighted (by the SELECT function followed by cursor movement keys).

The examples below include (1) changing the first character of a word to upper case, (2) changing all the characters of a word to uppercase, and (3) changing all the characters of a word to lowercase.

```
CAPITALIZE  WORD

UPPERCASE  WORD

LOWERCASE  WORD
```

One of the most often used functions within any editor or word processor is the "global search and replace" function, where every occurrence of one text string is replaced by another text string. This may be done within EVE command level as follows, where the first text string is the text to search for, and the second is the text to be used as the replacement. Thus, every occurrence of "project a" is replaced with "project b."

```
REPLACE  "project  a"  "project  b"
```

Unlike many "search and replace" functions, this function within EVE provides the user with several additional options. Rather than immediately replacing the text described, following the REPLACE command, the user is allowed to enter the following responses for each occurrence of the search text found. Note the following display and explanations:

```
Buffer: FILE1.MEMO                          | Write | Insert | Forward
Replace? Type Yes, No, All, Lost, or Quit:
```

- • Y, for "yes," replace the current occurrence of the text and search for the next.

- • N, for "no," do not replace the current occurrence and search for the next.

- • L, for "last," replace the current occurrence but terminate the search for additional occurrences.

- • Q, for "quit," do not replace the current occurrence and terminate the search for additional occurrences.

- • A, for "all," replace the current and all additional occurrences immediately. Do not prompt the user at each occurrence.

Cut and Paste

We have already considered the "cut and paste" operation, along with variations, such as the COPY function, which may be performed from the editing keypad and the EDT keypad. Once again, command equivalents are available.

The SELECT, REMOVE and INSERT HERE functions available with the keys can be performed with the following EVE commands:

```
SELECT

REMOVE

INSERT  HERE
```

The RESET function, where the current select mark is removed, is performed with the following command:

```
RESET
```

The COPY function, where the highlighted text is inserted into the "cut buffer" without removing the text from the original location is as follows:

```
COPY
```

Text Alignment

There are several text alignment functions available within EVE. These may be summarized as follows:

- Center a line of text according to the current margins.

- Automatically wrap new text onto the next line when typing beyond the current margins.

- Justify or FILL text according to the current margins, although it was originally entered with different margin settings.

As can be seen from the above explanations, each of these functions is dependent upon the current margin settings. The default margin settings are column 1 for the left margin and column 80 for the right margin. These may be changed as follows:

```
SET LEFT MARGIN 5

SET RIGHT MARGIN 70
```

Once the margin settings are established, or the defaults are in effect, either the current line or all lines within the current region of text selected and highlighted may be centered according to the margin settings. This is done with the following command:

CENTER LINE

As new text is entered, text entered beyond the right margin may be automatically wrapped to the next line, without requiring the user to enter a RETURN. Word wrapping is enabled by default and may be disabled or enabled as follows:

```
SET NOWRAP

SET WRAP
```

Either the current paragraph or the entire region of text currently selected and highlighted may be justified or FILLed according to the current text margins by means of the following command:

```
FILL
```

Text Display

Most user terminals display 80 characters of text per line as the default and this is generally the width most comfortable to the eye. However, EVE permits entry of as many as 256 characters of text per line, although only 80 may be displayed. There are several methods of displaying text beyond the standard 80 character width:

- Change the line width on the terminal to more than 80 characters. Most terminals permit display of at least 132 character lines, although some loss of readability may occur at this width.

- Shift the 80 or 132 character view of the user any number of characters to the right, and back again to the left. This provides access to columns 81-256 without any loss of readability or in the event that the display terminal cannot work with lines beyond 80 characters.

The current line width displayed by the terminal may be changed with the following command. This assumes that the terminal device is capable of displaying the number of characters specified with the command.

```
SET WIDTH 132

SET WIDTH 80
```

With the current terminal width set either to 80 or 132 columns, and with text having been entered beyond that width, shift the user view of the document the specified number of characters to the right or left.

```
SHIFT RIGHT 50

SHIFT LEFT 50
```

Buffers

There are two basic types of buffers which are used within EVE, user buffers and system buffers. Our main concern within this section will be user buffers, although we will briefly explain system buffers also.

System buffers are created by EVE to store and display editor information. These buffers are usually read-only buffers that cannot be modified. For example, entering the HELP command at EVE command level will display a buffer of text listing all the EVE commands. This is an example of a system buffer which may be viewed, but cannot be changed.

User buffers are usually associated with specific files. When we name a particular file as we begin our editing session, the following takes place:

- An EVE user buffer is created and assigned the same name as the file specified.

- The file is loaded from the disk into the buffer.

- Any editing that we perform during the session is actually performed on the buffer, not the file.

- When we have completed the editing session, the EXIT function described earlier writes the contents of the buffer to the disk as a new version of the file. The QUIT function simply terminates the editing session without writing the buffer, thereby leaving the old version of the file as the latest on the disk and not saving the changes from the session.

When we enter EVE without naming a file for editing, a system buffer called MAIN is created and we are allowed to enter text within this buffer. When we exit EVE, we are prompted for a file name to use to save the contents of the buffer, and the MAIN buffer is written to the disk file specified.

As you should now understand, we have been using a single user buffer to edit a single sample file in the examples within this chapter. It is possible, though, to have several different user buffers within a single editing session, containing the data from several different disk files. By switching between buffers, one can edit several different files within a single editing session.

Once we have begun our EVE session, we have one buffer currently displayed, either the buffer for the file we are editing or the MAIN buffer (if we failed to name a file when we began the session). We may load additional files into buffers with the following commands:

```
GET  FILE  FILE1.MEMO

GET  FILE  FILE2.MEMO

GET  FILE  FILE3.MEMO
```

These commands each read the file indicated from the disk and load the contents into an EVE buffer that is assigned the same name as the disk file. Our original buffer, either MAIN or the buffer for the first file named when the editing session began, is still loaded, but the current buffer displayed is the one for the file most recently loaded. In our example above, this would be FILE3.MEMO.

You may examine the buffers that are loaded for the present EVE session with the following command:

```
SHOW  BUFFERS
```

The display lists the buffers currently available, the number of lines of text within each buffer, and whether or not the buffer has been modified during this session.

```
Buffer name              Lines  Attributes

  FILE1.MEMO                8  Modified
  FILE2.MEMO                2  Modified
  FILE3.MEMO                1  Modified




















  Buffer: BUFFER LIST Use SELECT to view or REMOVE to delete buffers
```

When the list of current buffers is displayed, the following options are available:

- The UP and DOWN ARROW keys permit you to scroll up and down through the display of available buffers.

- While the cursor is positioned at one of the buffers listed, pressing the SELECT key from the editing keypad will change the buffer from the one previously displayed to the one listed on the display line of the SHOW BUFFERS command.

- While the cursor is positioned at one of the buffers, pressing the REMOVE key from the editing keypad will delete the buffer from the editing session. If you attempt to delete a buffer to which modifications have been made, you are prompted for one of the following responses:

  - WRITE to write the buffer to the disk file before deletion
  - DELETE to delete the buffer only, without writing the

              modifications to disk
-    QUIT to cancel the just requested deletion of the buffer

If you can recall the names of the buffers you are working with, and you likely can in most cases, you can switch between buffers and delete buffers directly with the following commands. First, to change your current buffer displayed to a new buffer, enter:

```
BUFFER FILE2.MEMO
```

Your original buffer remains intact and available. However, the current buffer displayed is the one for FILE2.MEMO. Following edits to this buffer, we may use the BUFFER command again to switch to FILE1.MEMO, FILE3.MEMO or back to FILE2.MEMO again.

We considered earlier the "cut and paste" function and the different ways of implementing this function. There is a single "cut buffer" (not to be confused with our discussion here of buffers for files) that is shared among all the user buffers. Thus, text may be "cut" (REMOVE function) or "copied" (COPY function) from one buffer and inserted (INSERT HERE function) into another, thereby moving data between buffers. This is performed with the following steps:

1)   Select and highlight the text to be moved from the first EVE user buffer by positioning the cursor to the beginning of the text, pressing the SELECT key, and moving the cursor to highlight the desired text region.

2)   With the text from the first buffer selected and highlighted, insert the text into the "cut buffer" with either the REMOVE or COPY functions.

3)   Switch to the second EVE user buffer with the BUFFER command.

4)   Position the cursor to the desired location within the second buffer and use the INSERT HERE function to paste the text from the first buffer into the second one.

To delete a buffer, enter the command below. Once again, if the buffer has been changed, you are given the option of saving the changes to the corresponding disk file.

```
DELETE BUFFER FILE1.MEMO
```

Rather than loading a disk file into a buffer for editing, you may include the contents of a disk file within the current buffer you are editing. The following command includes the contents of the FILE2.MEMO file into the current buffer, inserting the text at the beginning of the buffer. The disk file FILE2.MEMO is not changed in any way.

```
INCLUDE FILE FILE2.MEMO
```

You may immediately write the contents of the current buffer to the disk without ending the editing session. The first command below writes the buffer to the disk file and creates a new version of the file being modified. The second command names a different file that is to be created using the contents of the current buffer.

```
WRITE FILE

WRITE FILE NEW_FILE.MEMO
```

When multiple buffers are in use and an EXIT function is invoked, the following steps occur:

- The current buffer is written to the disk, creating a new version of the file.

- The user is given the option to save all other user buffers that were modified but not displayed as the current buffer. A response of "Y" or "N" must be given in response to the prompt for each additional buffer.

Windows

At this point you can already appreciate the advantage and flexibility of using multiple buffers to edit several files within a single session. Even more useful, though, would be the option of displaying several of the current user buffers on the screen at the same time, being able to view other buffers while editing the current one. This is performed with EVE windows.

Your terminal screen may be divided up into several different windows. You may then load into each window any one of the user buffers. With the various buffers displayed in the screen windows, you may then switch between windows, editing the buffer within one window while displaying the buffers in the other widows.

As you know, EVE initially provides one window. You may split the screen into two windows with either of the following commands:

```
TWO  WINDOWS
SPLIT  WINDOW  2
```

With the SPLIT WINDOW command, you also have the option of splitting the screen into as many windows as will fit on the terminal device you are using. Notice the following example with the command SPLIT WINDOW 3 being entered while the buffer FILE1.MEMO is current.

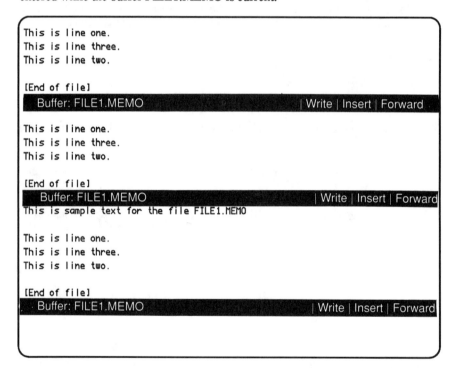

Although there are three windows, you will notice that all three have the current buffer FILE1.MEMO displayed, while our cursor is positioned at the top window. Our next step is to switch to the other windows and change the buffers that are displayed in each one. We can switch to another window with either of the following commands:

```
NEXT  WINDOW
PREVIOUS  WINDOW
```

While the cursor is positioned at the second window, we may then switch the buffer for the window to FILE2.MEMO with either the BUFFER FILE2.MEMO command (if the file was already loaded into a buffer) or the GET FILE FILE2.MEMO (if we had not already loaded the file into a buffer). We can switch to the last window and perform the same function for FILE3.MEMO.

Having created three windows and loaded three separate buffers into each, we may now edit one buffer and switch to another while all three are displayed. We move between buffers by using the NEXT WINDOW or PREVIOUS window commands, as we have shown. Similarly, we can "cut and paste" between buffers as considered earlier.

When we split one window into three, all three windows are of the same size. While we are positioned within one of the windows as our current window, we may enlarge or shrink the size of that window, taking or adding lines from adjacent windows. The following commands enlarge and shrink the current window by the number of lines stated:

```
ENLARGE WINDOW 5

SHRINK WINDOW 5
```

We may also delete the current window from the screen. The buffer contained within the window is still loaded within memory, and we may still switch to that buffer at a later time. However, the window and its display of the buffer will be removed.

```
DELETE WINDOW
```

Finally, we may delete all the windows except the current one and return to using a single window. Again, the buffers from the other windows are still loaded within memory and may still be accessed later with the BUFFER or SHOW BUFFERS command.

```
ONE WINDOW
```

Initialization and Command Files

We have briefly considered DCL command procedures in an earlier chapter. As mentioned, any valid DCL command that we may enter interactively may be added to a list of commands within a text file. The command procedure may then be executed (using the @ command), thereby executing each command within the procedure automatically.

EVE supports command files for a similar purpose. Any EVE command that can be entered at command level (following the DO key) may be added to an EVE command file and the entire sequence of commands executed at once.

There are only a few syntax rules for EVE command files:

- The EVE command must be entered within the text file exactly the same as if we entered the command from the EVE interactive command level.

- Only one command may be entered per line.

- Comment lines may be inserted if prefaced by an exclamation mark (!).

As an example of a command file within EVE, recall the previous section where we modified three separate files within three windows on the screen. We could perform all the set up for this operation by creating a command file named THREE_WINDOWS.EVE as follows:

```
! Split the screen into three separate windows
SPLIT WINDOW 3

! With the first and current window, load file 1
GET FILE FILE1.MEMO

! Switch to the next window; load file 2
NEXT WINDOW
GET FILE FILE2.MEMO

! Switch to the next (third) window; load file 3
NEXT WINDOW
GET FILE FILE3.MEMO
```

Once we have first begun our editing session, we may execute the command procedure to load all three files into the appropriate window by entering the following command after the DO key:

```
@THREE_WINDOWS.EVE
```

Thus, whenever you wish to work with the three files FILE1.MEMO, FILE2.MEMO and FILE3.MEMO, you may simply invoke the command file with the EVE @ command at EVE command level and have EVE execute the commands from the procedure.

You may have various EVE commands that you wish to execute each time you invoke the EVE editor and begin a new editing session. This is similar in concept to the DCL procedure LOGIN.COM, which executes every time you begin a DCL session.

By creating an EVE command file that contains the functions we wish to perform for each EVE session, we can initialize the EVE environment to meet our preferences.

For example, while we may have several different command files to perform specific functions, such as shown above, there may be the following commands that we wish to perform to initialize every EVE session, regardless of which files we may subsequently access:

```
! Activate EDT keypad emulation
SET KEYPAD EDT

! Set customized margins
SET LEFT MARGIN 10
SET RIGHT MARGIN 70

! Specify other customization functions
SET CURSOR BOUND
SET NOWRAP
```

When EVE is first invoked, initialization command files may be automatically executed in the following ways:

- By adding the qualifier /INITIALIZATION to the DCL command EDIT/TPU, we specify a command file to be used for this EVE session for initialization. For instance, we could have the THREE_WINDOWS.EVE procedure execute automatically as an initialization procedure for an EVE session by using the command below:

  $ EDIT/TPU/INITIALIZATION=THREE_WINDOWS.EVE

- If we have not named a specific initialization file with the EDIT/TPU/INITIALIZATION command, EVE will search the current default directory for a file named EVE$INIT.EVE. If a file so named is found, it will automatically invoke that procedure as an initialization file.

- If the file EVE$INIT.EVE is not found within the current default directory, a search is made for the same file name within the main-level directory (as indicated by the logical name SYS$LOGIN), and this EVE command file is executed if found.

- If none of the above conditions are met, EVE will lastly attempt to translate the logical name EVE$INIT. If the user has equated an EVE command file name to the logical name EVE$INIT (with the DEFINE command) and the file can be found, it is used as the initialization file.

Thus, we may create various initialization files for different types of editing sessions and store the files within an appropriate subdirectory. For instance, we may create an initialization file name EVE$INIT.EVE within the [.MEMOS] subdirectory that contains specific initialization commands for editing our memo files. We may create another initialization file within the other subdirectories which pertain to the type of files stored there. If there is no EVE$INIT.EVE file within a particular subdirectory, we may create an overall default EVE$INIT.EVE file within the top-level directory. And finally, if for a particular editing session we wish to use a special command file as an exception, we can name that file with the EDIT/TPU/INITIALIZATION command and override the other initialization files.

If we specifically do not want to use an initialization file that may otherwise be invoked automatically, we may use the /NOINITIALIZATION qualifier as follows:

```
$ EDIT/TPU/NOINITIALIZATION
```

Advanced Functions

To complete our discussion of EVE, we will consider the following advanced features that are most useful:

- User-defined function keys that we may equate to any EVE function and use similarly to the standard EVE and EDT function keys.

- Executing DCL commands from within an EVE session.

- Recovering lost data when an EVE session is terminated or the system crashes before the current buffers are written to their corresponding disk files.

User-Defined Function Keys

By now you should be quite familiar with the execution of certain EVE commands by using the EVE and EDT function keys which are available. There may be additional EVE commands that you use quite frequently which are not available from one of the function keys. EVE allows for the definition of user function keys, where most function keys or control keys can be equated to specific EVE commands of your choice. You may then press the key to invoke the function.

For example, suppose that we often entered the following commands to create and remove multiple windows on our screen:

```
SPLIT WINDOW 3

ONE WINDOW
```

We can equate each of these commands to a function key, perhaps F17 and F18, by entering the following commands at EVE command level. We may then simply press the appropriate function key to execute the command.

```
DEFINE KEY=F17 SPLIT WINDOW 3

DEFINE KEY=F18 ONE WINDOW
```

If we have activated EDT keypad emulation (and therefore the GOLD or PF1 key available with EDT), we may also include the GOLD key combination when defining user function keys. For instance, we could modify the above example to use the F17 function key to split the screen into three windows while using the GOLD F17 function key to revert back to a single window. The GOLD key combinations are specified as follows:

```
DEFINE KEY=F17 SPLIT WINDOW 3

DEFINE KEY=GOLD-F17 ONE WINDOW
```

DCL Commands Within EVE

There may be cases where you need to invoke a DCL command while you are working within an EVE session. For example, you may need a list of file names available by using the DIRECTORY command, or you may wish to view the current list of interactive users with the SHOW USERS command. EVE permits the execution of DCL commands without leaving the EVE session or interrupting the editing currently being performed.

This may be performed as follows:

- Press the DO key to enter EVE command level.

- Preface the DCL command with the EVE command DCL and enter any DCL command, as follows:

  DCL DIRECTORY/SIZE

  DCL SHOW USERS

Once a DCL command is entered in this manner, the following actions take place:

- A subprocess is spawned and the command is executed.

- A read-only window with the name DCL is created on the screen. The output from the command is output into the DCL window.

- Subsequent DCL commands append the additional output to the end of the same DCL buffer.

Once the DCL output has been included within the DCL buffer, the data within the buffer may be accessed by the user similar to data in any other read-only buffer. For example, the following actions may be performed:

- Any cursor movement keys, such as PREVIOUS SCREEN and NEXT SCREEN, may be used to view the data within the DCL window.

- Data may be "copied" from the DCL buffer and inserted into one of the user buffers.

- When the DCL window is no longer required, you may remove the window by entering the ONE WINDOW command or the DELETE WINDOW DCL command.

Recovering A Session

If the EVE session is terminated abnormally (such as from a system crash or the user pressing the CONTROL Y key inadvertently and causing an interrupt), the modifications from the EVE session will not be applied to the text file and the data will be lost. This problem is avoided by EVE by means of the TPU journal log.

As an EVE session is in progress, the TPU editor saves all the key strokes from the user session in a log file. When the session is terminated normally, and the changes from the session are correctly applied to a new version of the file, the journal file is automatically deleted. Thus, you may rarely ever see this file within your directory.

In the event that the session is terminated abnormally, the changes are not applied to the file and the journal file is not deleted. Notice in the example the abnormal termination of an EVE session as the user presses the CONTROL Y (interrupt) key.

```
This is the text for the file FILE1.MEMO.  At this point we are going to
enter the CONTROL Y key to abort the file
   Interrupt

$
```

Notice next how the DIRECTORY command confirms that the journal file FILE1.TJL exists.

```
$ DIRECTORY FILE1

Directory $DISK1:[SMITH]

FILE1.MEMO;1         FILE1.TJL;1

Total of 2 files.
$
```

The name of the journal file is assigned according to the following rules:

- The file is created within the current user default directory.

- The file is assigned the name of the original input file specified within the EDIT/TPU command, with a file name extension of .TJL.

- If no original file name is used with the EDIT/TPU command, the file name TPU.TJL is used.

- The default naming of the journal file may be overridden by using the /JOURNAL qualifier to specially name a journal file, as follows:

```
$ EDIT/TPU/JOURNAL=JOURNAL.TJL FILE1.MEMO
```

- The creation of a journal file may be avoided altogether with the /NOJOURNAL qualifier. (While this would marginally improve the performance of your editing session, obviously this would also eliminate the opportunity to recover any changes if the session was aborted).

To recover a session by using the .TJL file, include the /RECOVER qualifier with the EDIT/TPU command. The command during the recovery operation must be identical to that specified when the file was first invoked, with the exception of the /RECOVER qualifier. Note the example below to recover a session that began with the command EDIT/TPU/JOURNAL=JOURNAL.TJL FILE1.MEMO.

```
$ EDIT/TPU/JOURNAL=JOURNAL.TJL/RECOVER FILE1.MEMO
```

You will observe on your screen that during the recovery the .TJL file is retrieved and the key strokes automatically applied against the most recent version of the data file. Once the recovery is complete, you may then exit the session normally and the edits will have been recovered and saved.

Chapter 8 Exercises

Perform the following exercises in order to become familiar with the various EVE features that we have considered.

Any function that involves the use of the GOLD (or PF1) key or any of the numeric keypad keys will not work unless EDT keypad emulation has been set up. You may remember that EDT keypad emulation is not invoked by default. Therefore, be sure that you preface any use of these keys within an EVE session by entering the SET KEYPAD EDT command either interactively or within a command file. This must be done every time a new EVE session is started from DCL.

Also, remember that the DO key must be pressed to receive the command prompt and enter EVE commands. The command may be terminated by using either the DO key again or pressing the RETURN key.

Also, EVE commands, like DCL commands, may be abbreviated and need not be entered in their entirety.

Exercise 1
EVE Keypad Functions

a) Invoke the EVE editor with a sample file named FILE1.MEMO and enter sample text. Switch the text entry mode to overstrike (F14 function key) and modify the text. Use the DELETE key to delete characters where necessary.

b) Use the EVE keypad functions for cursor movement:

- ARROW keys
- PREV SCREEN
- NEXT SCREEN

c) Perform a FIND operation using the FIND key on the editing keypad. Do the following:

- Find text
- Find the next occurrence with a "double FIND"
- Reverse the direction with F11 and perform a reverse FIND

d) Use the EVE function key operations:

- MOVE BY LINE
- ERASE WORD
- EXIT

e) Do a "cut and paste" operation using the SELECT, REMOVE and INSERT HERE function keys as described within this chapter.

f) Set up the numeric keypad to emulate the EDT keypad with the command SET KEYPAD EDT.

g) Using the diagram of the EDT keypad and the explanations within this chapter, perform the following functions:

- Delete a line and restore ("undelete") the line. Do the same for a word and a character.

- Perform a "cut and paste" operation using the SELECT, CUT (REMOVE) and PASTE (INSERT HERE) keys from the EDT keypad.

- Attempt any additional functions desired from the EDT keypad.

Exercise 2
Cursor Movement

a) Perform the BOTTOM and TOP functions of EVE in the following manner:

- GOLD DOWN arrow (BOTTOM) and GOLD UP arrow (TOP) keys
- GOLD 4 (BOTTOM) and GOLD 5 (TOP) keys from the EDT function (numeric) keypad
- BOTTOM and TOP commands entered at EVE command level

b) Insert several page breaks throughout the document by positioning the cursor to the desired point and entering the command INSERT PAGE.

c) Use the following cursor movement functions:

- MOVE BY WORD
- MOVE BY LINE
- MOVE BY PAGE

Exercise 3
Basic Editing Features

a) Use the ERASE and RESTORE commands to erase and restore portions of text within the document.

b) Select a region of text using the SELECT function and cursor movement keys and attempt the following commands while the text is highlighted:

- CAPITALIZE WORD
- UPPERCASE WORD
- LOWERCASE WORD

c) Use the REPLACE command to perform a "search and replace" operation.

Exercise 4
Text Alignment

a) Set the left and right margins of your document to columns 5 and 50 respectively with the SET LEFT MARGIN and SET RIGHT MARGIN commands.

b) Once the margins are set, press the RETURN key to create a new line of text and begin entering the text. Note the alignment of the text according to the new margin settings.

c) Use the CENTER LINE command to center the line of text at the current cursor position according to the margin settings.

d) Select a region of text that was entered using the original, default margin settings of columns 1 and 80. Select and highlight the text by using the SELECT function and the cursor movement keys. Once the text is selected, align the text according to the new margin settings with the FILL command.

Exercise 5
Buffers And Windows

a) Select three files that you wish to use for this exercise. If you wish, you may quickly create three small text files named FILE1.MEMO, FILE2.MEMO and FILE3.MEMO that contain any junk text.

b) Invoke the editor and name the first file with the command EDIT/TPU FILE1.MEMO.

c) Load the remaining files into buffers with the GET FILE command.

d) Using either the SHOW BUFFERS command to list all available buffers, or the BUFFER command to directly switch buffers, switch from the current buffer to another buffer.

e) Perform a "cut" operation (SELECT, cursor movement keys, REMOVE commands) from one buffer, switch to another buffer (BUFFER or SHOW BUFFERS commands), and perform a "paste" (INSERT HERE) operation.

f) Split the screen into three windows with the SPLIT WINDOW 3 command.

g) Using the NEXT WINDOW or PREVIOUS WINDOW commands, switch to another window.

h) In the other window, use either SHOW BUFFERS or the BUFFER command to display a second buffer in the window.

i) Switch to the third window (NEXT WINDOW or PREVIOUS window commands) and display the third buffer within that window (SHOW BUFFERS or BUFFER commands).

Exercise 6
Command Files

a) Using the EVE editor, create a command file named THREE_WINDOWS.EVE that contains the commands to automatically split the screen into windows and load the appropriate files. You may use the example included within this chapter or create a similar procedure with your own commands.

b) Using the DCL command EDIT/TPU/INITIALIZATION=THREE_WINDOWS.EVE, invoke the command file when starting a new EVE session.

c) Within your top-level directory, use the EVE editor to create a command file named EVE$INIT.EVE and include the following initialization commands, along with any others that you prefer. Then, invoke the command file automatically for the next EVE session by simply entering the command EDIT/TPU.

```
SET  KEYPAD  EDT
SET  LEFT  MARGIN  5
SET  RIGHT  MARGIN  70
```

Be sure that the command file is named EVE$INIT.EVE and is stored within your initial default top-level directory (as indicated by the logical name SYS$LOGIN). Otherwise, the command file will not be automatically invoked with the EDIT/TPU command alone.

Exercise 7
Advanced Functions

a) Define two function keys to perform EVE commands, using the DEFINE KEY command. Then use the function keys to verify that they have been correctly defined.

b) Add these same function key definitions within the EVE initialization file already created so that the definitions are automatically performed for every EVE session.

c) Use the DCL command within EVE to create a DCL window and execute any DCL command. Try the following command as one example:

```
DCL  DIRECTORY/SIZE/DATE
```

d) Abort the session by pressing the CONTROL Y key. Use the DIRECTORY command to verify that a .TJL journal file has been created.

e) Recover the aborted session by entering the command
    EDIT/TPU/RECOVER along with any other qualifiers and file
    name specified when the session was originally started.

    Be sure that the EDIT/TPU command during the recovery is
    precisely the same as the one used for the initial session that was
    aborted, with the exception of the /RECOVER qualifier.

    Following the recovery, exit the session normally and note the
    successful recovery.

Exercise Answers

Many of the exercises within this chapter involve pressing various function keys as directed within the exercise instructions. The answers to such exercises cannot be stated in writing as we have done in earlier chapters. Thus, many of the exercises do not have answers for this reason. For such exercises, follow the instructions carefully and refer to the sample screen snapshots included within the chapter itself.

However, where possible, answers for some of the exercises have been included.

Exercise 4a

```
SET  LEFT  MARGIN  5
SET  RIGHT  MARGIN  50
```

Exercise 5a

```
$ EDIT/TPU  FILE1.MEMO
^ Z
$ EDIT/TPU  FILE2.MEMO
^ Z
$ EDIT/TPU  FILE3.MEMO
^ Z
```

Exercise 5b

```
$ EDIT/TPU  FILE1.MEMO
```

Exercise 5c

```
GET  FILE  FILE2.MEMO
GET  FILE  FILE3.MEMO
```

Exercise 6a

```
$ EDIT/TPU THREE_WINDOWS.EVE

! Split the screen into three separate windows
SPLIT WINDOW 3

! With the first and current window, load file 1
GET FILE FILE1.MEMO

! Switch to the next window; load file 2
NEXT WINDOW
GET FILE FILE2.MEMO

! Switch to the next (third) window; load file 3
NEXT WINDOW
GET FILE FILE3.MEMO
^ Z
```

Exercise 6b

Self-explanatory

Exercise 6c

```
$ EDIT/TPU [SMITH]EVE$INIT.EVE

SET KEYPAD EDT
SET LEFT MARGIN 5
SET RIGHT MARGIN 70
^ Z

$ EDIT/TPU FILE1.MEMO
```

Exercise 7a

```
SET KEYPAD EDT
DEFINE KEY=F17 SPLIT WINDOW 3
DEFINE KEY=GOLD-F17 ONE WINDOW
```

Exercise 7b

Self-explanatory

Exercise 7c

Self-explanatory

Exercise 7d

```
$ EDIT/TPU JUNK.FILE
 . . .
^ Y
$ DIRECTORY JUNK.TJL
```

Exercise 7e

```
$ EDIT/TPU/RECOVER JUNK.FILE
```

Chapter Nine

Mail and Phone

Overview

VMS provides two very powerful and convenient utilities that permit communication between users, known as MAIL and PHONE. Both of these utilities are among the most popular of all features available from VMS and its DCL interface.

The MAIL utility allows one user to create documents, messages or other files and transmit these to any other user on any VAX within the network of systems. The message is stored in a file for the receiving user, who may read the message at his or her convenience. The receiving user need not be logged on at the time the message is received.

The PHONE utility allows two users to immediately correspond with one another via their respective terminals. By establishing a PHONE session between two users, the text that they enter on their own terminal is immediately displayed on the other user's terminal. There can even be a "conference call" where several users all communicate with one another via their terminals. Obviously, a user must be currently logged on in order to participate in a PHONE session.

As with the MAIL utility, users from any VAX system anywhere within the network may communicate with other users via the PHONE utility.

You may remember from our earlier discussion of the SET command that messages from either the MAIL or PHONE utility may be blocked with any one of the following commands:

```
$ SET BROADCAST=(NOMAIL,NOPHONE)
        or

$ SET BROADCAST=(NONE)
        or

$ SET TERMINAL/NOBROADCAST
```

178

Within this chapter, we will first consider the features of the MAIL utility, followed by the PHONE utility.

MAIL Overview

Any document or text file that has been created by an editor or other means and is stored within a user's directory may be mailed to another user by means of MAIL. Additionally, a mail message may be interactively created from within the MAIL utility itself and then mailed to another user or group of users.

By default, there is a single file in the user's top-level directory called MAIL.MAI. While all mail messages are usually stored within this single file, the MAIL utility organizes individual messages within this file according to "folders." Users have the option of defining and using any number of folders to organize their messages.

Note

If you use the DCL DIRECTORY command to look for the MAIL.MAI file, it may not yet exist within your directory if you have never received any mail. However, it will be automatically created when you receive your first mail message.

In addition to any number of user-defined folders that may be created for a user, the MAIL utility will create and use the following folders automatically:

- NEWMAIL is the name of the folder that contains any messages that you have received but have not yet read (thus, the name NEWMAIL).

- MAIL is the name of the folder that contains messages that you have previously received and read. Once you read a new message from the NEWMAIL folder, the message is automatically moved out of the NEWMAIL folder and into the MAIL folder. Therefore, while there may or may not be any messages within the NEWMAIL folder at any given time, the MAIL folder will continue to accumulate mail messages as they are received and read.

- WASTEBASKET is the name of the folder that contains messages
  that you have deleted. As a safety feature, messages from any folder
  that you delete are not immediately deleted in a physical sense, but
  are moved out of the folder in which the message was stored and
  into the WASTEBASKET folder. There is a period of time, as
  discussed later within this chapter, when deleted messages contained
  within the WASTEBASKET folder are retained and may be moved
  out of the folder and back into the original folder, thereby undoing
  the delete operation.

There is a separate command level that is available when using the utility. This
is identified with a unique prompt. Note the following example where the MAIL
utility is invoked from DCL with the MAIL command and the special MAIL
prompt is displayed.

```
$ MAIL

MAIL>
```

We will consider throughout this chapter the various MAIL commands that may
be entered at this prompt. When a particular MAIL session is complete and the
user wishes to return to DCL command level, this may be done with either the
EXIT command of MAIL or the CONTROL Z key.

```
MAIL> EXIT
$
```

Note

Some of the MAIL concepts and commands are very similar, if
not identical, to some of the DCL concepts and commands we
have discussed, although their precise function is obviously
quite different. In order to avoid becoming confused between
the two concepts and commands of MAIL and DCL, notice
carefully the prompt which indicates in which command level
you are currently working. When at DCL command level, as
indicated by the dollar sign ($) prompt, only DCL commands
may be entered. When at MAIL command level, as indicated
by the MAIL> prompt, only MAIL commands may be
entered.

Note (continued)

Also similar to DCL, all MAIL commands may be abbreviated to as few characters as would make them unique among other commands. Even ambiguous commands which are too brief to distinguish them among others, such as only entering a single character, may be entered. This is not recommended, however, as the ambiguous entry of the commands may not signify the specific command that you think will be invoked.

Within our examples for MAIL, as within the rest of the textbook, abbreviations are not used simply for the purpose of clarity in the examples. However, feel free to use abbreviations in your own work.

As is true with other utilities and DCL itself, there is extensive on-line documentation available for the MAIL utility. For help on any of the commands or other functions available, enter the HELP command at the MAIL prompt.

```
To obtain information about all of  the  MAIL  commands,  enter  the
following command:

    MAIL> HELP *

To obtain information about individual  commands  or  topics,  enter
HELP followed by the command or topic name.

  Format:

    HELP [topic]


Additional information available:

/EDIT       /PERSONAL_NAME      /SELF     /SUBJECT   ANSWER    ATTACH
BACK        COMPRESS    COPY    CURRENT    DEFINE     DELETE    DIRECTORY
EDIT        ERASE       EXIT    EXTRACT    FILE       FIRST     Folders
FORWARD     GETTING_STARTED     HELP       KEYPAD     LAST      MAIL
MARK        MOVE        NEXT    PRINT      PURGE      QUIT      READ
REMOVE      REPLY       SEARCH  SELECT     SEND       SET-SHOW  SPAWN
V5_CHANGES

Topic?
```

Within the sections that follow for the MAIL utility, we will consider the following topics:

- Sending mail to one or more users with the MAIL or SEND commands.

- Reading mail that has been sent to you from another user with the READ command.

- Scanning through messages with the CURRENT, BACK, NEXT, FIRST and LAST commands.

- Searching for text within a message with the SEARCH command.

- Responding to a mail message that you have received with the REPLY or ANSWER commands.

- Forwarding the message that you have received to a third party with the FORWARD command.

- Switching the context of your mail session from one folder to another with the DIRECTORY and SELECT commands.

- Organizing mail messages within folders using the FILE or MOVE and the COPY commands.

- Deleting messages with the DELETE command.

- Several additional functions available within the MAIL utility.

- Customizing the mail environment using the various options of the SET command, and viewing the current setting of those options with corresponding SHOW commands.

- Using the MAIL function keypad.

MAIL
SEND

A mail message is comprised of two basic sections: (1) the message header, and (2) the actual message text itself. The following items comprise the message header for a mail message:

- The return or FROM address. This is the node name and user name of the one sending the message. If we are sending a message, our local VAX node name and our own user name is the return address.

- The recipient or TO address. This is the node name and user name of one or more recipients of the message.

- The carbon copy or CC address. This is the node name and user name of one or more additional recipients of the message, which are included within a carbon copy list. By default, a CC list is not provided. CC lists are discussed later within the chapter.

- The SUBJECT. This is a very brief, optional message that we may include within the header of the mail message to briefly describe the message contents. A SUBJECT is useful to the recipient so that they may easily identify the message from among all messages received.

There are basically three different methods by which we can create a message to be mailed. These are:

1) Create a text file by means of an editor or other program or utility and use the MAIL utility to send the file.

2) Within the MAIL utility, create a message with very limited editing capabilities.

3) Also within the MAIL utility, select an editor (such as EVE or EDT) and create a message using all the features of the selected editor from within the MAIL utility.

Using the first method, assume that we have already created a text file named STATUS.REPORT using the EVE editor. We may mail the message to JONES on our own local VAX by using the DCL command MAIL. Notice that the first parameter states the file name specification and the second parameter identifies the user name of the recipient of the message. The return address will automatically be set to our own VAX node name and our own user name.

```
$ MAIL STATUS.REPORT JONES
```

If no error message is displayed, we may assume that the message was correctly sent.

We may use the /SUBJECT qualifier to include a brief subject message along with the mail message itself.

```
$ MAIL -
/SUBJECT="January report" STATUS.REPORT JONES
```

This basic command may be enhanced in several ways. If the text file was not stored within our default directory, naturally we could simply be more specific by using a more complete file name specification. Or, if the user JONES was located on the VAX node name EARTH:: rather than our own local system, then we must include the node name along with the user name when addressing the message. And finally, if we wished to send the message to several individuals, we could do so by naming a parameter list of users. The following command demonstrates these enhancements.

```
$ MAIL [SMITH.MEMOS]STATUS.REPORT EARTH::JONES, -
VAX1::WILSON,VAX2::HARRIS
```

In addition to the subject that we may append for a message, we may also include a more descriptive "return address" on our message to supplement our own node name and user name. This additional message is specified with the /PERSONAL_NAME qualifier. When the recipient receives the message and is notified of the node name and user name that sent the message, they will also see the personal name that we have included.

```
$ MAIL -
/PERSONAL_NAME="John Smith x5522" STATUS.REPORT -
  EARTH::JONES,VAX1::WILSON
```

We may desire a copy of the message we are sending within our own mail file. The /SELF qualifier sends a copy of the message to you. The message is included within your NEWMAIL folder, the same as the recipients of the message.

```
$ MAIL -
/SELF STATUS.REPORT EARTH::JONES,VAX1::WILSON
```

Rather than having to create a file before using the MAIL utility, we may use the second method outlined above, using a limited editor to create a message within MAIL itself. When in the utility, enter the SEND or MAIL command (the two are synonymous).

When creating a message interactively, we are prompted for the recipient address and the subject.

```
/MAIL> SEND
To:     SIDERIS
Subj:   Interactively created message
Enter your message below. Press CTRL/Z when complete, or CTRL/C to quit:
This is a brief message that we will send
  Exit
```

As the notice displayed by MAIL states, we complete the message and send it to the recipient by pressing the CONTROL Z key. Or we may cancel the message while we have started creating the text and not send it after all by pressing the CONTROL C key and return to the MAIL prompt.

Similar to creating a file with the DCL command CREATE, when creating a message in this manner, our editing features are limited. While we may use the line editing keys (LEFT and RIGHT ARROW, DELETE, etc.) once we have pressed the RETURN key and begun another line, we cannot go back and edit a previous line.

When creating a message interactively, we may also use the /PERSONAL_NAME and /SELF qualifiers with the SEND or MAIL command.

```
MAIL>  SEND/SELF/PERSONAL_NAME="John  Smith,VAX"
```

The /CC qualifier allows a carbon copy list to be created when sending the message. The carbon copy list contains the node name and user name addresses of additional recipients of the message. We are prompted for the CC list after we have entered the other portions of the message header.

```
/MAIL> SEND/CC
To:     HOWARD
CC:     HOLLAND
Subj:   Sample message including CC list of one user
Enter your message below. Press CTRL/Z when complete, or CTRL/C to quit:
```

The third, and perhaps best, method of sending mail allows the user to utilize one of the editors when creating the message. First, we must select the editor that we want with the SET EDITOR command.

```
MAIL>  SET  EDITOR  TPU
```

```
MAIL> SET EDITOR EDT
```

As we will see later within this chapter, all SET commands within the MAIL utility are permanent settings. Thus, once we have SET the option desired, it remains set even after we have terminated the MAIL session and terminated the DCL session.

Having selected the editor of our choice, we may now use the SEND/EDIT (or the synonymous MAIL/EDIT) command to create a message from within the MAIL utility but utilizing the editor and all its features.

```
MAIL> SEND/EDIT
```

After we complete the header portions of the message, the editor is invoked for us to create the message text. While using the editor, we may use all the same functions as with any other editing session. To complete the message and send it to the recipient, use the EXIT command. To abort the message and not send it to the recipient, use the QUIT command.

We may, of course, use the /SELF, /PERSONAL_NAME or /CC qualifiers along with the /EDIT qualifier.

Our final option when sending mail involves the use of distribution lists. If we regularly send mail to a group of users, we may create a distribution list file that contains their addresses. Whenever sending mail to this group, we may reference the distribution list rather than entering their individual node name and user name addresses each time.

For example, suppose that our status report messages are always sent to the same group of users. We could use the CREATE command or one of the editors to create the following text file that contains the addresses. (The CONTROL Z or ^Z key is used to terminate the CREATE command and return to DCL level.)

```
$ CREATE STATUS.DIS
! First line of the distribution list, a comment line
! Another comment line, prefaced by exclamation mark
VAX1::THOMPSON
VAX2::MARINO
VAX3::BROWN        ! Joseph Brown from Home Office
^ Z

$
```

When sending the status report, we may address JONES and WILSON on our
local system, along with all the individuals included within the distribution list.

```
MAIL> SEND
To: JONES, WILSON, @STATUS.DIS
```

The following simple rules exist for the creation and use of distribution lists
within the MAIL utility of VMS:

- The node name and user name address within the distribution list
  should be stated in exactly the same format as when stating the
  address interactively from within the MAIL utility.

- Comments may be included within the file by using the
  exclamation mark (!). Comments may be separate lines or added at
  the end of an address line. Both cases are shown in the example
  above.

- Multiple distribution lists may be included by using a parameter
  list of addresses for the message, such as the following:

  To: @STATUS.DIS, @BOSSES.DIS, VAX1::BROWN

- Within the distribution list we may reference another list by again
  using the @ command.

- When using the distribution list, if some of the addresses are
  incorrect, the utility will provide the option of sending the mail
  anyway to the remaining users.

  We are informed of which node name and user name address are
  invalid, and must respond with either a Y or N to indicate whether
  or not we want to send the message to remaining, valid addresses.

  Note the example that follows where the invalid user name JUNK
  has been included in the distribution list that we have specified.

```
%MAIL-E-NOSUCHUSR, no such user JUNK
Do you want to send anyway (Y/N, default is N)?
```

READ

When a user has received mail, it is automatically inserted within the NEWMAIL folder. Users are informed of any new mail that they receive in the following ways:

- If the user is logged on when the message is received, a notification message is immediately broadcast on the recipient's screen. The notification message includes the node name/user name address of the sender, along with the personal name used by the sender, if any, and the current time.

  (Recall that such messages may be blocked with the SET BROADCAST=(NOMAIL) or the SET TERMINAL/NOBROADCAST commands.)

- When the user first logs in, the VMS login process displays the number of messages, if any, currently contained within the NEWMAIL folder.

- When the user begins a new mail session by entering the DCL command MAIL, the number of messages, if any, currently contained within the NEWMAIL folder is displayed.

- At any time within the MAIL session the user may view the current count of new mail messages with the command SHOW NEW_MAIL_COUNT.

To illustrate, note the sample broadcast message displayed at the time the message is received.

```
New mail on node SI860B from ZDTICO::SIDERIS       "Dan Sideris, Sideris Consulti
ng, (508) 651-3800" (11:01:34)
```

Or, note the message automatically displayed at the time of login.

```
        Welcome to VAX/VMS version V5.1-1 on node SI860B
    Last interactive login on Wednesday, 13-SEP-1989 10:59
    Last non-interactive login on Wednesday, 10-AUG-1988 22:54

        You have 1 new Mail message.
```

A similar message is displayed whenever a MAIL session is begun.

```
$ MAIL

You have 1 new message.

MAIL>
```

Finally, the same message is displayed when the user requests the count with the SHOW NEW_MAIL_COUNT command.

The DIRECTORY command within MAIL lists the messages contained within one of the folders specified. We may view this list of the NEWMAIL folder by entering the command DIRECTORY NEWMAIL or simply DIRECTORY, which defaults to the NEWMAIL folder if there is any new mail. (A complete section regarding the DIRECTORY command within MAIL is included later within this chapter).

The display that follows shows the NEWMAIL folder of the recipient of a message received from SIDERIS on node ZDTICO::.

```
                                                              NEWMAIL
   # From                Date        Subject

   1 ZDTICO::SIDERIS     13-SEP-1989  Sample message

MAIL>
```

We may sequentially read our new mail with any of the following commands:

- Entering the READ/NEW command.

- Entering the READ command, which will default to reading the new messages, if there are any.

- Simply pressing the RETURN key, which will also default to reading the new messages, if there are any.

Note the following example where the user begins reading new mail by using any one of the above methods.

```
  #1            13-SEP-1989 11:01:33.84                            NEWMAIL
From:  ZDTICO::SIDERIS        "Dan Sideris, Sideris Consulting, (508) 651-3800"
To:    SIDERIS
CC:
Subj:  Interactively created message

This is a brief message that we will send

MAIL>
```

While reading the new messages, we may simply press the RETURN key to continue reading all new mail, until we are informed that there are no new messages.

Once we have read all of the new mail, it is automatically moved out of the NEWMAIL folder and into the MAIL folder. Thus, the NEWMAIL folder is empty. However, the MAIL folder contains the messages that were originally stored within the NEWMAIL folder.

Rather than sequentially reading the messages within the NEWMAIL folder, we may select individual messages by stating the message number as follows:

```
    MAIL>  READ  3
    MAIL>  READ  2
    MAIL>  READ  1
```

Even the READ command itself is optional. We could simply enter the message number, with the READ command being implied.

```
    MAIL>  3
```

We may also read messages from any other folder, such as the older messages contained within the MAIL folder. There are several ways in which this may be performed.

First, if there are no unread messages, and therefore there is no NEWMAIL folder, the utility will assume a default of the MAIL folder. Thus, by simply entering the READ command or just pressing the RETURN key, we will sequentially read the older messages from the MAIL folder. Or we may selectively read messages from this folder by naming the message number.

```
    MAIL>  READ  3
```

If there is a NEWMAIL folder, and this is assumed by the utility as the default folder, we must explicitly identify both the folder name and the message number if we wish to read a message from a folder other than the default NEWMAIL folder. This is done by adding the folder name along with the message number to the READ command.

```
MAIL>  READ MAIL 3
```

We will consider later within this chapter other methods of reading messages that are not in the current default folder. This is done by changing the default to another folder.

CURRENT
BACK / NEXT
FIRST / LAST

Thus far, we have considered two methods in which you may read and select a message within a folder, either sequentially (by simply pressing the RETURN key successively) or directly (by naming the message number with the READ command such as READ 2).

When sequentially reading through messages within a folder, you may wish to move to the following locations within the folder:

- Go back to the beginning or first page of the current message. The current message may be quite long and contain several pages.

- Go back to the previous message.

- Go back to the first message within the folder.

- Go forward past the current message, which may be quite long, to the next message within the folder.

- Go forward to the last message within the folder.

To go back to the beginning of the current message that you are reading, enter the following command. This will display the first page of the current message. We may again read successive pages of the message by just pressing the RETURN key.

```
MAIL>  CURRENT
```

To go back to the first page of the previous message within the folder, enter:

```
MAIL>  BACK
```

To go back to the first message within the folder, enter:

```
MAIL>  FIRST
```

To skip over the current message, which may be quite long and be displayed over several screen pages, enter the following command to go forward to the next message within the folder:

```
MAIL>  NEXT
```

Finally, to move forward to the last message within the folder, enter:

```
MAIL>  LAST
```

The messages that you select and read with these commands may be several pages long. If you would prefer to review the messages within the control of the editor, you may do so. For each of these commands, CURRENT, FIRST, LAST, etc., you may append the /EDIT qualifier. This selects the message desired, but also loads the message within the editor, allowing you to read the message using the cursor movement functions provided within the editor.

For example, if we again wished to select the last message within the folder, but wanted to view the message using the editor currently selected with the SET EDITOR command, we could do so as follows:

```
MAIL>  LAST/EDIT
```

By way of a reminder at this point, remember that abbreviations are valid for all of the MAIL commands. Hence, we may use the abbreviations CUR for CURRENT, BA for BACK, and so on. This is equally true for all the MAIL commands within this chapter, including those already discussed as well as those that follow in subsequent sections.

SEARCH

The search command allows the user to specify a string of text to search for and begins a search of the messages within the current folder. The first message found that contains the search text will be displayed.

Note the following example where we search for the first occurrence of "problem" within a message of the current folder:

```
MAIL> SEARCH problem
```

While enclosing the text you wish to search for within quotation marks (" ") is not always required, it is good practice to do so. Further, if we wanted to search for text that included several words, we would have to enclose the text within quotes. Notice the example that follows:

```
MAIL> SEARCH "problem with the new person hired"
```

If you wish to search for the next message that contains the same search string, simply enter the SEARCH command without specifying any search text. The search will begin with the next message and display the first message thereafter that contains the search text.

REPLY
ANSWER

When reading a message, we may reply or answer the message by using either the REPLY or ANSWER command (the two are synonymous).

The utility will not ask for the node name and user name address of the recipient of this message as it uses the return address of the message you are reading. It will also not prompt you for a subject, as it uses the same subject on the original message. You simply enter the reply and send the response by pressing CONTROL Z.

In the example that follows, the user has selected and is viewing a brief message received from the user SIDERIS on the VAX node name ZDTICO::. A reply may be sent back to the originator of the message as follows:

```
  #1              13-SEP-1989 11:12:15.57                              MAIL
From:    ZDTICO::SIDERIS      "Dan Sideris, Sideris Consulting, (508) 651-3800"
To:      SIDERIS
CC:
Subj:    Sample message

a

MAIL> REPLY
To:      ZDTICO::SIDERIS
Subj:    RE: Sample message
Enter your message below. Press CTRL/Z when complete, or CTRL/C to quit:
```

When creating the reply, you again have the option of using the editor you have selected with the SET EDITOR command by appending the /EDIT qualifier to REPLY or ANSWER.

```
    MAIL>  REPLY/EDIT
```

Similarly, when we are creating a message with the REPLY command, we have the SAME qualifiers available which we used with the SEND command. Their function is similar to that already described.

These qualifiers are as follows:

- /CC
- /PERSONAL_NAME
- /SELF

FORWARD

When reading a message from another user, we may forward the message to a third party by using the FORWARD command. This command will not prompt us for the message text, as we are forwarding a message already received. We are simply prompted for the third party's address and a subject we may wish to include.

In the next example, the user JONES is reading a message that has been received from SMITH. The user JONES decides to forward the message to a third party, WHITE.

```
   #1              13-SEP-1989 13:22:36
From:   EARTH::SMITH
To:     JONES
Subj:   January status


Dear Mr. Jones:

The status of the January project is as follows...

MAIL> FORWARD
To:     WHITE
Subj:   Please note report from SMITH that is attached

MAIL>
```

The third party that receives the message may in turn forward the message to another user.

Whenever someone receives a message that originated from one user but was forwarded by another, the message header includes an audit trail describing where the message originated and the forwarding users. Note the following message header received by WHITE:

```
   #1              13-SEP-1989 13:24:57
From:   EARTH::JONES
To:     WHITE
Subj:   Please note report from SMITH that is attached

From:   EARTH::SMITH      13-SEP-1989 13:22
To:     JONES
Subj:   January status


Dear Mr. Jones:

The status of the January project is as follows...
```

Rather than forwarding a message that we have received verbatim, we may wish to edit the message before forwarding it. This may be done with the /EDIT qualifier. The editor we have selected is invoked, the message text that we are reading is loaded into the editor buffer, and we may use the features of the editor to modify the text before forwarding it to the third party.

```
MAIL>  FORWARD/EDIT
```

DIRECTORY
SELECT

In addition to the standard folders created and used by the MAIL utility, such as the NEWMAIL, MAIL and WASTEBASKET folders, recall our earlier mention of user-defined folders that may also be created. Within this section we will consider the MAIL commands that pertain to the use of both standard and user-defined folders.

We may view all the folders that currently exist within our MAIL file, including any user-defined folders, with the DIRECTORY/FOLDERS command. For instance, if we have both unread new mail and older mail already read, we should have both the NEWMAIL and MAIL folders within our file.

```
MAIL> DIRECTORY/FOLDERS
Listing of folders in DUA0:[JONES]MAIL.MAI;1
     Press CTRL/C to cancel listing
MAIL                                    NEWMAIL

MAIL>
```

We may obtain a listing of the messages within a folder with the DIRECTORY command.

```
MAIL>  DIRECTORY  NEWMAIL
MAIL>  DIRECTORY  MAIL
```

The DIRECTORY command lists the following information for each message:

- The name of the folder being listed
- The number of the message within the folder
- The node name/user name return address of the sender
- The date the message was received
- The subject text assigned by the sender

```
                                                            MAIL
 # From              Date        Subject

 1 EARTH::SMITH      13-SEP-1989  January status
 2 EARTH::SMITH      13-SEP-1989  February status
 3 EARTH::SMITH      13-SEP-1989  Problem highlighted during last meeting
 4 EARTH::SMITH      13-SEP-1989  Problem resolved after discussion with W
 5 EARTH::SMITH      13-SEP-1989  Upcoming meeting

MAIL>
```

In the prior section we mentioned the default folders that the MAIL utility assumes, namely the NEWMAIL folder if there is any unread mail, or the MAIL folder if there is no unread mail. When reading messages from a folder that is not the current default, you must explicitly identify the folder name along with the message number, as demonstrated in the prior section.

```
MAIL> READ MAIL 3
```

Similar to the manner in which we changed our assumed default disk directory within DCL, we may also change the default folder assumed by MAIL. Whenever we use the DIRECTORY command as shown above to list the messages within a folder, this also changes the assumed default folder to the one just listed. Thus, if we enter the command DIRECTORY MAIL, the MAIL folder is now the assumed default folder.

If we wished to read message number three from this folder, or obtain a directory listing of all the messages within the folder, we may simply enter the following commands, even though there may be a NEWMAIL or other user-defined folders. This is because our default folder has been set and this is the folder assumed by MAIL.

```
MAIL> READ 3

MAIL> DIRECTORY
```

We may also explicitly change the default folder with the SELECT command.

```
MAIL> SELECT MAIL
```

Any MAIL command used will now assume the MAIL folder as the current default, until we terminate the MAIL session or change the default folder again.

Thus far we have used the DIRECTORY command to list all of the messages contained within the current folder. However, there are a number of qualifiers which may be used to limit the messages displayed with the command.

Messages within the current folder that are included within the directory listing may be chosen based upon the following criteria:

- All messages received either before or since a certain date, using the /BEFORE or /SINCE qualifiers.

- All messages that have been marked with the MARK command using the /MARKED qualifier. (The MARK command is considered later within this chapter).

- All messages for which you have sent a reply with the REPLY or ANSWER command using the /REPLIED.

- All messages that contain certain text within the various portions of the header of the mail message:

    - The FROM (return address) portion of the header using /FROM
    - The TO (recipients address) portion of the header using /TO
    - The SUBJECT portion of the header using /SUBJECT
    - The CC (carbon copy) portion of the header using /CC

- Messages starting with a certain message number within the folder using the /START qualifier.

To include within the listing all messages received either before or since the date of January 1, 1990, we would enter either the first or the second command listed below. Note how the VMS date format already considered for DCL commands is followed within the MAIL utility.

```
MAIL> DIRECTORY/BEFORE=01-JAN-1990
```

                          or

```
MAIL> DIRECTORY/SINCE=01-JAN-1990
```

To include within the listing only those messages that have been marked, enter the following:

```
MAIL> DIRECTORY/MARKED
```

To include those messages for which we have sent a reply, enter the following:

```
MAIL> DIRECTORY/REPLIED
```

To include within the listing all messages within the folder with a FROM (return) address, TO address, or CC address of EARTH::JONES, enter:

```
MAIL> DIRECTORY/FROM="EARTH::JONES"
                   or
MAIL> DIRECTORY/TO="EARTH::JONES"
                   or
MAIL> DIRECTORY/CC="EARTH::JONES"
```

To include all messages where a reference to "accounts payable" is made within the subject of the message header, enter:

```
MAIL> DIRECTORY/SUBJECT="accounts payable"
```

To begin the directory listing with a certain message number within the folder, such as the fifth message, enter the following:

```
MAIL> DIRECTORY/START=5
```

Finally, regardless of which folder we have currently selected, we may use the DIRECTORY command to provide a listing of the messages within the NEWMAIL folder that have yet to be read.

```
MAIL> DIRECTORY/NEW
```

FILE
MOVE

Thus far, we have referred several times to user-defined folders. Within this section we will create and use such folders to organize our mail messages.

Suppose that over the course of time we have received many messages and these have accumulated within the MAIL folder. We may wish to create several folders of our own choosing and move some of the messages out of the MAIL folder and into our own folders. For example, rather than having all of the status reports that we have received stored within our MAIL folder, we may wish to create separate folders for JANUARY, FEBRUARY, and so on, and move the corresponding status reports into these folders.

In order to do this, we must identify the message to be moved by selecting the folder and the specific message.

```
MAIL> SELECT MAIL
MAIL> READ 2
```

Having selected message number 2 within the MAIL folder as our current message, we may use either the FILE or the MOVE command (the two are synonymous) to move the message out of the MAIL folder and into a new folder named JANUARY.

```
MAIL> FILE JANUARY
Folder JANUARY does not exist.
Do you want to create it (Y/N, default is N)? Y
%MAIL-I-NEWFOLDER, folder JANUARY created

MAIL>
```

Notice that when we reference a folder that does not already exist, the utility allows us to first create the folder before moving the message.

We may now view the messages currently stored within the MAIL and JANUARY folders.

```
MAIL> DIRECTORY MAIL
MAIL> DIRECTORY JANUARY
```

Also, the DIRECTORY/FOLDERS command also indicates that a new folder named JANUARY has been created.

We may repeat this function for as many messages as we wish to move out of the MAIL folder and into other user-defined folders.

Messages contained within a user-defined folder may likewise be moved out into any other folder, whether it be another user-defined folder or one of the standard folders, such as MAIL.

This is done in the same manner as discussed before. Suppose that we wanted to move the first message now contained within the JANUARY folder back into the MAIL folder. We must first select the message within the JANUARY folder with either of the following two methods:

```
MAIL> SELECT JANUARY
MAIL> READ 1

MAIL> READ JANUARY 1
```

With the correct message now selected, either the MOVE or FILE commands will move the message back into the MAIL folder.

```
MAIL> MOVE MAIL
```

Note

Whenever a folder is emptied of all the messages it contained, the folder itself is also deleted. Thus, if we empty the JANUARY folder of its messages by means of the MOVE command or others yet to be discussed, the DIRECTORY/FOLDERS command will show that the folder itself has been deleted. If we later wish to move messages into the JANUARY folder once again, it must be re-created in the same manner as when we first created the folder.

This is also true of standard folders such as NEWMAIL, MAIL, etc. If there is no unread mail, the NEWMAIL folder will not exist and will not be displayed with the DIRECTORY/FOLDERS command.

By default, all folders, both standard and user-defined, are stored within the MAIL.MAI file in your disk directory. If we prefer, we may store the user-defined folders within a separate subdirectory and file. This is done when the folder is created.

To illustrate, if we were moving a file to a new .folder that will be created, and we wanted to create the folder within a special subdirectory called [SMITH.MAIL] and with a unique name, we could append this file specification after the MOVE or FILE command.

```
MAIL> MOVE JANUARY [SMITH.MAIL]JANUARY.MAI
```

Note

By default, the file name extension assigned to any files created for folders is .MAI. It is recommended that you use this same default file name extension for these files by either not stating any file name extension (and thereby receiving the default extension name of .MAI) or using the extension .MAI if one is explicitly stated, as shown in the above example.

Also note that while the disk file indicated will be created if one does not already exist, the subdirectory must have already been created with the CREATE/DIRECTORY command.

If it is necessary to move all of the messages within a folder, this may be done with the /ALL qualifier. The next example selects the MAIL folder and moves all of the messages out of the folder and into the JANUARY folder.

```
MAIL> SELECT MAIL
MAIL> MOVE/ALL JANUARY
```

COPY

Rather than moving a message out of a folder and into another folder, as just discussed, we may instead want to create a copy of the message within a folder, while leaving the message within its original folder as well. This is done with the COPY command.

Suppose that we once again wanted to select the second message within the MAIL folder and store it within the JANUARY folder. However, we wanted to create a copy within the JANUARY folder while leaving the message within the MAIL folder also.

First, we must select the message with either of the following commands:

```
MAIL> SELECT MAIL
MAIL> READ 2
```

```
        or
```

```
MAIL> READ MAIL 2
```

We then may use the COPY command, naming the folder in which the message should be copied.

```
MAIL> COPY JANUARY
```

Identical to the MOVE or FILE commands, if the folder that we identify does not exist, the user is given the option of first creating the folder. When creating the folder, we may name another subdirectory and file.

The /ALL qualifier is likewise available for the COPY command. We may thus copy all of the messages within the selected folder.

DELETE

This command deletes a message from the current folder. As explained during the introduction for this chapter, the message is initially not deleted but rather moved into a folder named WASTEBASKET. Normally, the WASTEBASKET folder will retain all deleted messages from all folders until the user terminates the MAIL session and returns to DCL command level by entering the EXIT command. Once the MAIL session is terminated, the WASTEBASKET folder is purged and the messages physically deleted from the file. (There are several commands that alter the default processing of the WASTEBASKET. These are considered later within the chapter).

As with most other MAIL commands, we must first select a folder and a message within that folder before working with it, such as for a delete operation. The following command demonstrates one of the methods we have discussed to select the fourth message within the MAIL folder.

```
MAIL> READ MAIL 4
```

To delete the message currently displayed, we can simply enter the DELETE command.

```
MAIL> DELETE
```

While the DIRECTORY listing of the messages within the MAIL folder indicates that the message was deleted, a similar listing of the WASTEBASKET folder shows that the message actually remains on file, but has been moved to the WASTEBASKET.

```
                                                          WASTEBASKET
    # From              Date         Subject

    1 EARTH::SMITH      13-SEP-1989  Problem resolved after discussion with W

MAIL>
```

At this point, we could enter the EXIT command to terminate the MAIL session and physically delete the messages within the WASTEBASKET. However, if we decided to restore the message back within its original folder, we could use the MOVE command as already discussed to move the message out of the WASTEBASKET folder and back into the MAIL folder.

```
MAIL> READ WASTEBASKET 1
MAIL> MOVE MAIL
```

The message has now been moved back into the MAIL folder, and terminating the session will not delete the message.

We may delete several messages within a folder with a single DELETE command. In the next example, we select the MAIL folder once again. Rather than reading or selecting a single message within the folder and then deleting it, we use a parameter list with the DELETE command to delete several messages directly.

```
MAIL>  SELECT  MAIL
MAIL>  DELETE  1,3,5
```

We may delete a range of messages within a folder, such as messages one through five, with either of the following syntax:

```
MAIL>  SELECT  MAIL
MAIL>  DELETE  1-5
```

```
        or
```

```
MAIL>  DELETE  1:5
```

Finally, we may use the /ALL qualifier to delete all of the messages within the folder. Remember that once a folder is emptied of all its messages, the folder itself ceases to exist and must be re-created at a later time if it is to be used again.

```
MAIL>  SELECT  MAIL
MAIL>  DELETE/ALL
```

EXTRACT

We may wish to extract a message from out of the mail file and into a text file of its own. This is done with the EXTRACT command. Either the entire message, including the message header that contains the FROM address, TO address, etc., or simply the message text itself may be extracted.

As usual, we must first select the folder and the message to be extracted. In our example, message number 2 is selected from the JANUARY folder.

```
MAIL>  SELECT  JANUARY
MAIL>  2
```

With the message selected and displayed, we use the EXTRACT command along with the file specification that we wish to use to contain the message. The message is copied from the folder and stored within the text file named. Both the message header and the message text are extracted.

```
    #2              13-SEP-1989 13:30:16
  From:   EARTH::SMITH
  To:     JONES
  Subj:   Problem resolved after discussion with WHITE


  MAIL> EXTRACT PROBLEM.MEMO
  %MAIL-I-CREATED, DUA0:[JONES]PROBLEM.MEMO;1 created

  MAIL> Exit
  $ TYPE PROBLEM.MEMO
  From:   EARTH::SMITH          13-SEP-1989 13:30
  To:     JONES
  Subj:   Problem resolved after discussion with WHITE

  $
```

We may extract only the message text, without the header information with the /NOHEADER qualifier.

```
    MAIL> EXTRACT/NOHEADER PROBLEM.MEMO
```

The /ALL qualifier is available for the EXTRACT command. We extract all of the messages within the folder selected.

The /MAIL qualifier formats a MAIL file, with a .MAI extension, as the output file, rather than a text file. This MAIL-formatted file may be used at a later time as an external folder file, as described with the MOVE, FILE and COPY commands.

PRINT

It may be necessary for us to print one of the messages within the mail files to a print queue. We could do this by using the EXTRACT command to create a copy of a message within a DCL text file and then use the DCL print command to send the text file to one of the print queues. The MAIL PRINT command allows us to perform the same function directly from the MAIL utility.

Once we have selected a folder and a message within the folder, we may schedule the message for printing on the default print queue SYS$PRINT with the following command:

    MAIL> PRINT

The message is not immediately submitted to the queue for printing but saved within a buffer for your mail session. Each message that you request printing for within the session is added to this buffer. When the mail session is terminated with an EXIT command, all the messages scheduled for printing within the buffer are submitted as a single entry within the queue.

We may request that a message be scheduled immediately as an entry within the queue before the MAIL session is terminated with either the /NOW or /PRINT qualifier (the two are synonymous) of the PRINT command.

    MAIL> PRINT/NOW

                or

    MAIL> PRINT/PRINT

The /ALL qualifier is available for the PRINT command. We schedule for printing all of the messages within the folder selected.

When scheduling a message for printing, the following qualifiers for the MAIL PRINT command are available, similar to the DCL PRINT command. The qualifiers perform the same function as when scheduling a DCL text file for printing with the DCL PRINT command.

- /AFTER
- /HOLD
- /NOTIFY
- /COPIES
- /BURST
- /FLAG
- /TRAILER
- /QUEUE

MARK
UNMARK

The MARK command allows us to mark a message for later reference. This mark is especially useful with the additional options of the SELECT command, considered in the next section.

Of the messages contained within the MAIL folder, we may wish to mark the first and third messages for later reference.

We may mark the messages by first selecting the folder (which was implicitly done above when the DIRECTORY command was entered) and then identifying the message number to be marked.

```
MAIL>  MARK  1
MAIL>  MARK  3
```

The listing of the message after the mark is as follows:

```
                                                                    MAIL
      # From             Date        Subject

 *    1 ZDTICO::SIDERIS  13-SEP-1989 Sample message
      2 ZDTICO::SIDERIS  13-SEP-1989 Large message
 *    3 ZDTICO::SIDERIS  13-SEP-1989 Important message

MAIL>
```

To unmark a message that has previously been marked, use the UNMARK command once the correct folder has been selected.

```
MAIL>  UNMARK  3
```

All messages within the current folder may be marked with the /ALL qualifier. We may then use the UNMARK command to selectively unmark a few messages within the folder, leaving the remaining ones marked.

SELECT

We briefly considered the SELECT command earlier during our discussion of folders. By using the SELECT command and naming a folder, we reset the current default folder and, in effect, select all the messages within the folder. Thus, we may use the /ALL qualifier of the COPY, FILE, etc., commands to operate on all of the messages within the folder selected.

The SELECT command also includes several optional qualifiers that allow us to select a subset of messages within a folder. Having selected just this subset of messages within the folder, we may then use the /ALL qualifier with the various commands considered and operate on only the subset of messages within the folder, rather than all messages within the folder.

This subset of messages within a folder may be selected based upon the following criteria:

- All messages received either before or since a certain date.

- All unread messages within the NEWMAIL folder.

- All messages that have been marked with the MARK command.

- All messages for which you have sent a reply with the REPLY or ANSWER command.

- All messages that contain certain text within the various portions of the header of the mail message:

    - The FROM (return address) portion of the header
    - The TO (recipients address) portion of the header
    - The SUBJECT portion of the header
    - The CC (carbon copy) portion of the header

To illustrate, suppose that we wished to use the MOVE/ALL command to move all of the messages within the MAIL folder that have been marked to the folder JANUARY. Assuming that we have marked the messages within the MAIL folder, we could select only the marked messages within the MAIL folder as follows:

```
MAIL> SELECT/MARKED MAIL
```

The DIRECTORY command would then list only those messages selected, that is, the marked messages.

We may now use the MOVE/ALL command, with the /ALL qualifier now indicating only those messages that have been selected, rather than actually all of the messages.

```
MAIL> MOVE/ALL JANUARY
```

Or, with only the marked messages selected, we could use the EXTRACT/ALL command. Rather than extracting all of the messages within the folder, as the /ALL qualifier would normally indicate, we extract only the messages selected with the SELECT/MARKED command.

```
MAIL> EXTRACT/ALL ALL_MESSAGES.TEXT
```

The /ALL qualifier is available with the following commands that we have considered:

- MOVE or FILE
- COPY
- SEARCH
- DELETE
- EXTRACT
- PRINT

To select all messages within the MAIL folder received either before or since the date of January 1, 1990, we would enter either the first or the second command listed below. Having selected such messages, we may again use any of the above listed commands that support the /ALL qualifier to operate on these messages.

```
MAIL> SELECT/BEFORE=01-JAN-1990 MAIL
```

```
                        or
```

```
MAIL> SELECT/SINCE=01-JAN-1990 MAIL
```

To select all messages within the folder with a return address of EARTH::JONES, enter:

```
MAIL> SELECT/FROM="EARTH::JONES" MAIL
```

To select any messages addressed to EARTH::JONES, enter:

```
MAIL> SELECT/TO="EARTH::JONES" MAIL
```

To select all messages where EARTH::JONES was specified on the carbon copy list, enter:

```
MAIL> SELECT/CC="EARTH::JONES" MAIL
```

To select all messages where a reference to "accounts payable" is made within the subject of the message header, enter:

```
MAIL> SELECT/SUBJECT="accounts payable" MAIL
```

QUIT
PURGE

The PURGE and QUIT commands both affect the way the WASTEBASKET folder is processed and, hence, the processing of deleted messages.

You are aware that deleted messages are actually moved to the WASTEBASKET, where they are held until the user terminates the MAIL session with the EXIT command. At this time, the messages are physically deleted and the WASTEBASKET is empty. The messages within the WASTEBASKET may be retained even after the MAIL session terminates with the QUIT command.

```
MAIL> QUIT

$
```

The session terminates and the user returns to DCL command level. However, when the next MAIL session begins, the deleted messages within the WASTEBASKET folder are still retained and may now be moved back into other folders if desired.

Conversely, the deleted messages within the WASTEBASKET folder may be immediately purged, even before the MAIL session terminates. This is done with the PURGE command.

```
MAIL> PURGE
```

COMPRESS

Over the course of time many messages may be deleted, new messages received, folders created and deleted, and so on. As a result, the internal organization of the MAIL may become quite fragmented. While this does not cause any errors or interfere with your ability to send and receive messages, you may notice that the utility works slower and performance begins to suffer.

A solution is the use of the COMPRESS command. This command reorganizes the MAIL.MAI file, reusing any wasted space resulting from the maintenance of messages, and thereby improving performance.

The example below illustrates the compress process, which usually takes no more than several seconds to complete.

```
MAIL> COMPRESS
%MAIL-S-CREATED, USER01:[SIDERIS]MAIL_CC05_COMPRESS.TMP;1 created
%MAIL-S-COPIED, USER01:[SIDERIS]MAIL.MAI;1 copied to USER01:[SIDERIS]MAIL_CC05_C
OMPRESS.TMP;1 (6 records)
%MAIL-S-RENAMED, USER01:[SIDERIS]MAIL.MAI;1 renamed to USER01:[SIDERIS]MAIL.OLD;
1
%MAIL-S-RENAMED, USER01:[SIDERIS]MAIL_CC05_COMPRESS.TMP;1 renamed to USER01:[SID
ERIS]MAIL.MAI;1

MAIL>
```

If we have created additional MAIL files, such as for our folders, the same problem may result with these files. We may compress these other files as well, simply by adding the file specification of the folder file as a parameter to the COMPRESS command.

```
MAIL> COMPRESS [SIDERIS.MAIL]JANUARY.MAI
```

If there is any system or disk device failure during the compress operation, or perhaps other problems, it is conceivable that the mail file could become corrupted and we would lose the record of some of our messages. In anticipation of such a potential problem, the COMPRESS operation first creates a backup copy of the mail file with the name MAIL.OLD. Thus, should the newly reorganized mail file become corrupted for any reason, we may simply rename the MAIL.OLD file back to the original mail file name and restore the valid record of our messages.

While we are considering the internal organization of the mail message file, we should mention the possible existence of secondary mail files. Depending upon the size of the messages that you have received, you may have noticed within your directory certain files with a long file name and an extension of .MAI. If a particular mail message that you receive is especially lengthy, the MAIL utility may decide to store the message as a separate file with a date and time stamp as the file name and .MAI as the file name extension. There is an internal pointer from the main MAIL.MAI file to the secondary file.

You continue to access this message as any other, as we have discussed throughout this chapter. The fact that the message text itself is stored in a secondary file is transparent and largely inconsequential. However, this explanation will help you to understand the existence of these files should they appear within your directory.

ERASE

The ERASE command simply clears the screen.

```
MAIL>  ERASE
```

SET
SHOW

We have the opportunity to use the various options for the SET command to customize the MAIL environment according to our own preferences. These preferences are recorded within a single control file used for all users on the VAX system (or perhaps cluster of VAX systems). Due to the fact that these preferences are recorded within this control file, they remain in effect after the MAIL or DCL session is terminated and need not be continually reset.

Each of the options available with the SET command may be displayed with the SHOW command. The options that we will consider for SET and SHOW are as follows:

- EDITOR
- PERSONAL_NAME
- COPY_SELF
- CC_PROMPT
- AUTO_PURGE
- FOLDER
- FORWARD
- MAIL_DIRECTORY
- QUEUE

- WASTEBASKET_NAME
- NEW_MAIL_COUNT

We may use the ALL option of the SHOW command to view all of the above
parameters that are set.

```
MAIL> SHOW ALL
Your mail file directory is USER01:[SIDERIS].
Your current mail file is USER01:[SIDERIS]MAIL.MAI;1.
Your current mail folder is MAIL.
The wastebasket folder name is WASTEBASKET.
Mail file USER01:[SIDERIS]MAIL.MAI;1
        contains 0 deleted message bytes.

You have 0 new messages.

You have not set a forwarding address.
Your personal name is "Dan Sideris, Sideris Consulting, (508) 651-3800".
Your editor is TPU.
CC prompting is enabled.
Automatic copy to yourself on SEND,REPLY.
Automatic deleted message purge is enabled.
Your default print queue is SYS$PRINT.
You have not specified a default print form. ˙

MAIL>
```

SET EDITOR

We discussed the SET EDITOR command at the beginning of this chapter. This
command allows us to specify which editor should be called when the /EDITOR
qualifier is used for the SEND or MAIL, REPLY or ANSWER, or FORWARD
commands.

```
MAIL> SET EDITOR TPU
MAIL> SET EDITOR EDT
```

SHOW EDITOR

The SHOW EDITOR command displays the current editor we have selected with the SET EDITOR command.

SET PERSONAL_NAME

We discussed the /PERSONAL_NAME qualifier and its purpose of appending an additional name to the return address of the message we are sending. We may establish a default personal name that will automatically be used whenever a message is sent.

```
MAIL> SET PERSONAL_NAME "John Smith - VAX group"
```

The text for the personal name is also displayed to the recipient as part of the notification message broadcast on the screen when the mail message is first received.

The /PERSONAL_NAME qualifier may still be used for an individual message being sent to override the default personal name.

The command SET NOPERSONAL_NAME removes the default personal name that has been set.

SHOW PERSONAL_NAME

This command displays the default personal name set for the user.

SET COPY_SELF

We discussed the use of the /SELF qualifier for the SEND or MAIL, REPLY or ANSWER, and FORWARD commands to send a copy of the message being mailed to our own NEWMAIL folder.

We may automatically receive such copies by default by entering the following command. Copies may be requested either when performing a SEND, REPLY or

FORWARD, or all of the above, as shown in the example.

```
MAIL> SET COPY_SELF SEND, REPLY, FORWARD
```

Having entered the above command, all messages that are sent will automatically send a copy to our own NEWMAIL folder. This may be avoided by using the /NOSELF qualifier with the SEND, REPLY or FORWARD commands at the time the message is actually being sent.

The automatic copy to oneself may be reversed with the following SET COPY_SELF command.

```
MAIL> SET COPY_SELF NOSEND, NOREPLY, NOFORWARD
```

SHOW COPY_SELF

This command displays which operations, if any, will automatically generate a copy of the message to you.

SET CC

We discussed the use of the /CC qualifier for the SEND or MAIL, REPLY or ANSWER, and FORWARD commands to allow us to enter a list of carbon copy addresses when sending a message.

The prompt for carbon copies may be automatically requested whenever a message is sent by entering the following command:

```
MAIL> SET CC
```

Having entered the above command, all messages that are sent will automatically include a CC list that we may create. This may be avoided by using the /NOCC qualifier with the SEND, REPLY or FORWARD commands at the time the message is actually being sent.

The automatic carbon copy prompting may be reversed with the following command:

```
MAIL> SET NOCC
```

SHOW CC

This command displays whether or not a carbon copy list is automatically generated when sending a message.

SET AUTO_PURGE

This command determines whether or not deleted messages will be automatically purged from the WASTEBASKET folder when the MAIL session terminates. As we have discussed, all deleted messages within the WASTEBASKET folder will be purged when the user terminates the MAIL session with the EXIT command. The messages will not be purged if the session is terminated with the QUIT command.

If the user records the SET NOAUTO_PURGE option within the mail control file, messages within the WASTEBASKET folder are not purged, even when the session terminates with the EXIT command.

```
MAIL> SET NOAUTO_PURGE
```

Thus, deleted messages will continue to accumulate within the WASTEBASKET folder indefinitely and will only be physically purged in one of the following ways:

- The user enters the PURGE command.

- The SET AUTO_PURGE command is entered and the user then terminates the session with the EXIT command.

To set up the automatic purge of the WASTEBASKET folder again, enter the following command. This is the initial default for MAIL.

```
MAIL> SET AUTO_PURGE
```

SHOW AUTO_PURGE

This command displays whether or not an automatic purge of deleted messages currently being held within the WASTEBASKET folder is performed or not.

SET FOLDER

This command is synonymous with the SELECT command. Recall that the SELECT command allows users to set the current default folder. Rather than using the SELECT JANUARY command to set the current folder, we could alternately use the following command:

```
MAIL> SET FOLDER JANUARY
```

The following qualifiers already discussed for the SELECT command provide identical functions for the SET FOLDER command.

- /MARKED
- /REPLIED
- /NEW
- /BEFORE or /SINCE
- /FROM
- /TO
- /CC
- /SUBJECT

The SET FOLDER command has been added as a synonym of the SELECT command to provide closer conformity to the DCL command syntax (such as the DCL SET DEFAULT command to change the current default directory). As we cautioned earlier, however, be certain not to confuse the valid MAIL commands that may be entered at the MAIL prompt with the valid, and quite similar, DCL commands that may be entered at the DCL prompt.

SHOW FOLDER

The SHOW FOLDER command displays the current default folder established by the user. SHOW FOLDER will display the current folder whether established with the SELECT or the SET FOLDER command.

SET FORWARD

As we stated at the outset of this textbook, VAX/VMS systems are often included within very extensive and sophisticated networks. You may actually have several different VAX systems on which you have authorized VAX/VMS user names and may work on several different systems over the course of a day or week.

If you are in an environment where you have authorized VAX/VMS user names on several different VAX systems, you are presented with a problem when it comes to checking whether you have received any MAIL messages from other users. If you have the SMITH user name authorized on three different VAX systems, namely VAX1::, VAX2:: and VAX3::, for example, you would have to log on to each system, watch for the new mail notification message that is displayed during the login process and then read any new mail within that account. The more systems that you have access to, the more systems that other users may correctly address mail to.

This problem can be avoided with the SET FORWARD command. This command allows you to specify an automatic forwarding node name and user name address for any mail that is addressed to the current account.

In our above example of accounts on VAX1::, VAX2:: and VAX3::, we could establish VAX3 as the node to receive all of the mail messages for all systems by setting a forwarding address on VAX1:: and VAX2:: as follows:

```
On  VAX1::
MAIL> SET FORWARD VAX3::SMITH

On  VAX2::
MAIL> SET FORWARD VAX3::SMITH
```

From this point forward, any messages addressed to VAX1::SMITH or VAX2::SMITH will be automatically forwarded to VAX3::SMITH. We now need only to log on to VAX3:: using the SMITH user name, and we can examine all messages that we may receive.

Use the following command to remove any forwarding address.

```
MAIL> SET NOFORWARD
```

SHOW FORWARD

This command displays whether or not a VAX MAIL forwarding address has been established for this user name.

SET MAIL_DIRECTORY

By default, the MAIL.MAI disk file used to store your mail messages is located within your default main-level directory (as indicated by the logical name SYS$LOGIN). Additionally, any other mail files that you may create for the folders are also stored within this same directory, unless stated otherwise at the time the folder file is created.

This command changes the default location of all MAIL files from your top-level directory to a subdirectory that you may name.

The following command states that the main MAIL.MAI mail file, and any other mail files that may be stored within the top-level directory, be moved to the subdirectory [.MAIL].

```
MAIL> SET MAIL_DIRECTORY [.MAIL]
```

A VMS subdirectory is created by means of this command.

The user may locate other non-MAIL files within this same subdirectory. It has no effect on MAIL.

SHOW MAIL_DIRECTORY

This command displays the current default directory or subdirectory used to store mail files. Initially, the default directory is the user's top level directory, as indicated by the SYS$LOGIN logical name.

SET QUEUE

Recall that the MAIL PRINT command allows the user to send one or more mail messages to a print queue for printing. Recall also that the print queue used by default is SYS$PRINT, unless the /QUEUE qualifier is used for the MAIL PRINT command to specify another available print queue.

The SET QUEUE command within MAIL allows the user to specify another queue as the default queue for the MAIL utility. Suppose for example, that the system manager had created a print queue named MAIL$PRINT and that we wished to set up this queue as the default queue for any printing of MAIL messages. We may do this with the following command.

```
MAIL> SET QUEUE MAIL$PRINT
```

We may still use the SYS$PRINT or any other print queue by using the /QUEUE qualifier on the MAIL PRINT command.

The following command restores the default queue assumed by MAIL to the SYS$PRINT print queue.

```
MAIL> SET NOQUEUE
```

Note

At the risk of being redundant, we again wish to remind the reader not to confuse MAIL and DCL functions. Establishing a default queue for the MAIL PRINT command has no effect on the DCL PRINT command. The DCL PRINT command will always use the queue name SYS$PRINT (unless the /QUEUE qualifier is used), regardless of what has been selected as the default queue within MAIL with the MAIL SET QUEUE command.

SHOW QUEUE

This command displays whether or not the user has selected a default print queue to be used for printing MAIL messages. If no default queue has been selected, MAIL will use the SYS$PRINT print queue for any messages printed with the MAIL PRINT command.

SET WASTEBASKET_NAME

This command allows the user to assign a name to the folder used by MAIL as the wastebasket to temporarily retain any deleted messages. By default, this folder is named WASTEBASKET.

The following command changes the name of the folder used as the wastebasket from WASTEBASKET to TRASH.

```
MAIL> SET WASTEBASKET_NAME TRASH
```

We may restore the name of the wastebasket folder to its original by entering the following command:

```
MAIL> SET WASTEBASKET_NAME WASTEBASKET
```

SHOW WASTEBASKET_NAME

This command displays the name of the folder used as the wastebasket. By default, this name is WASTEBASKET.

SHOW NEW_MAIL_COUNT

This command displays the number of unread messages currently contained within the NEWMAIL folder.

```
MAIL> SHOW NEW_MAIL_COUNT
```

MAIL Keypad

Our final topic for the MAIL utility pertains to the numeric keypad. Remember from our last chapter regarding the EVE editor that the numeric keypad keys were assigned to various editor functions (known as the EDT keypad).

A similar definition of the numeric keypad is done within the MAIL utility. Each of the keys is defined to invoke a certain MAIL function. Therefore, rather than entering the commands at the MAIL prompt, as we have learned throughout this chapter, we may simply press the appropriate key on the numeric keypad.

Also similar to the EDT keypad, each command is assigned two different functions. The top function listed is performed when the key is pressed. The bottom function is performed when the GOLD or PF1 key is pressed in combination with the function key.

The MAIL keypad diagram is as follows:

PF1	PF2	PF3	PF4
GOLD	HELP DIR/FOLD	EXT/MAIL EXTRACT	ERASE SEL MAIL
7 SEND SEND/EDIT	8 REPLY REP/ED/ EXT	9 FORWARD FOR/EDIT	- READ/NEW SHO NEW
4 CURRENT CURR/EDIT	5 FIRST FIRST/ED	6 LAST LAST/EDIT	, DIR/NEW DIR MAIL
1 BACK BACK/EDIT	2 PRINT PRIN/PRI N/NOTIFY	3 DIR DIR/START =99999	ENTER SELECT
0 NEXT NEXT/EDIT		. FILE DELETE	

The complete command names for each of these keys is as follows:

PF2	HELP
GOLD PF2	DIRECTORY/FOLDERS
PF3	EXTRACT/MAIL
GOLD PF3	EXTRACT
PF4	ERASE
GOLD PF4	SELECT MAIL
7	SEND
GOLD 7	SEND/EDIT
8	REPLY
GOLD 8	REPLY/EDIT

9	FORWARD
GOLD 9	FORWARD/EDIT
-	READ/NEW
GOLD -	SHOW NEW_MAIL_COUNT
4	CURRENT
GOLD 4	CURRENT/EDIT
5	FIRST
GOLD 5	FIRST/EDIT
6	LAST
GOLD 6	LAST/EDIT
,	DIRECTORY/NEW
GOLD ,	DIRECTORY MAIL
1	BACK
GOLD 1	BACK/EDIT
2	PRINT
GOLD 2	PRINT/PRINT/NOTIFY
3	DIRECTORY
GOLD 3	DIRECTORY/START=99999
0	NEXT
GOLD 0	NEXT/EDIT
.	FILE
GOLD .	DELETE
ENTER	SELECT

PHONE Overview

The PHONE utility provides for communication between users similar to the MAIL utility. Unlike MAIL, which allows users to communicate at different times by means of MAIL messages, the PHONE utility provides for immediate communication between two or more users. A user must be currently logged in in order to participate in a PHONE session.

There are two ways in which the utility may be used, either directly from DCL or at the PHONE command level from within the PHONE utility. We will illustrate these two ways within this section. To enter the PHONE utility from DCL, enter the following command:

```
$  PHONE
```

To exit from the PHONE utility and return to DCL level, enter the PHONE command EXIT or press the RETURN key.

Similar to the rest of the DCL environment, extensive on-line help is available from the PHONE utility by entering the HELP command from within PHONE command level. Note the following display:

```
                    ┌─────────────────────────┐
                    │  VAX/VMS Phone Facility  │            13-SEP-1989
  %                 └─────────────────────────┘
Press any key to cancel the help information and continue.
------------------------------------------------------------------------
HELP

The HELP command allows you to obtain information about the PHONE facility.
To obtain information about an individual command or topic, type HELP
followed by the command or topic name:

        HELP topic

HELP also accepts all of the other standard VMS help argument formats.

The information you request is displayed at your terminal until you type
any character at your keyboard.


Additional information available:

ANSWER      Characters DIAL      DIRECTORY  EXIT        FACSIMILE  HANGUP
HELP        HOLD       MAIL      REJECT     Switch_hook            UNHOLD
```

We will consider the following functions of the PHONE utility:

- Dialing another user.
- Answering a PHONE call from a user.
- Rejecting a PHONE call from a user.
- Ending a PHONE call with another user.
- FAXing a DCL text file to another user with the PHONE utility.
- Obtaining a directory listing of users.
- Establishing a conference call between several users.
- Unplugging the PHONE.
- Sending a brief MAIL message from PHONE.
- Putting a user on hold (and off hold).

PHONE
DIAL

We establish a PHONE session with another user by using their node name and user name address. If the user SMITH wished to place a call to the user JONES on the VAX node name EARTH::, the following DCL command would be entered.

```
$ PHONE EARTH::JONES
```

Alternately, the same function could be performed from the PHONE command level. Enter the utility by entering the PHONE command and pressing the RETURN key. The following display is provided. Note the percent sign (%) at the top of the display. This is the command prompt for the PHONE utility.

```
                   VAX/VMS Phone Facility            13-SEP-1989
 %

------------------------------------------------------------------
                         EARTH::SMITH




------------------------------------------------------------------
```

To place a call to a user once the PHONE utility has already been started, enter either the DIAL or PHONE command (the two are synonymous) at the PHONE percent sign prompt:

```
%  PHONE  EARTH::JONES

        or

%  DIAL  EARTH::JONES
```

The PHONE and DIAL commands are the assumed default commands within the utility. Thus, we could actually have placed the call by simply entering the node name and user name address, with the PHONE or DIAL command assumed.

```
%  EARTH::JONES
```

If JONES is not currently logged in or if his PHONE is unplugged, you will be notified with a message and must attempt to phone JONES at a later time. Otherwise, you will be informed that a PHONE call is ringing on JONES terminal and you must wait for his answer.

The phone call will ring indefinitely on JONES, terminal until he either answers or rejects the call. You may terminate the ringing by entering any key.

ANSWER

If a user has placed a phone call to you, as described in the last section, the following message is displayed on your terminal screen.

```
EARTH::JONES is phoning you on EARTH::      (16:26:01)
$
```

You may answer a PHONE call from DCL level by entering the following command:

```
$  PHONE  ANSWER
```

Alternately, we may enter the PHONE utility by entering the DCL command PHONE and pressing the RETURN key. Once we receive the display for the

PHONE utility, we may simply enter the ANSWER command itself at the percent sign prompt.

    %   ANSWER

Once we have answered the call, both users' PHONE display will include one section for text that you enter and another section for text the other user enters. Each of the users may simultaneously enter text to be displayed on the other user's terminal. Note the following display:

```
┌─────────────────────────────────────────────────────────────────────┐
│                  ┌─────────────────────────────┐                     │
│                  │   VAX/VMS Phone Facility     │     13-SEP-1989     │
│ %                └─────────────────────────────┘                     │
│                                                                       │
│ ------------------------------------------------------------------    │
│                             EARTH::SMITH                              │
│ Yes Jones, what can I do for you?                                     │
│                                                                       │
│                                                                       │
│                                                                       │
│                                                                       │
│                                                                       │
│ ------------------------------------------------------------------    │
│                             EARTH::JONES                              │
│ We need to meet at once regarding an urgent problem                   │
│                                                                       │
│                                                                       │
│                                                                       │
└─────────────────────────────────────────────────────────────────────┘
```

REJECT

When you receive a ringing message from another user, you may not wish to answer the call at this time. The ringing message will continue indefinitely, until the calling user terminates the ringing.

However, we may terminate the ringing message and reject the phone call by entering the following DCL command. This command invokes the PHONE utility, enters the REJECT command, exits the utility and returns to DCL level all with a single DCL command:

```
$ PHONE REJECT EXIT
```

Alternately, we could enter the PHONE utility and at the percent sign prompt of PHONE enter the REJECT command and then exit with either the EXIT command or the CONTROL Z key.

HANGUP

If we have answered a phone call and are currently conversing with another user, we may terminate the call or HANGUP the phone but remain within the utility and perhaps place a call ourselves to another user. This is performed with the HANGUP command.

While we are conversing with another user, to enter any PHONE command, including HANGUP, we must first press the percent sign (%) key. This indicates to PHONE that the next series of characters entered is *not* text to be displayed to the other user, but is a PHONE command.

After pressing the percent sign key, enter the following command.

```
% HANGUP
```

The phone call is ended, and we may call another user or enter the EXIT command to return to DCL level.

FACSIMILE

While we are conversing with another user in a PHONE session, we may wish to send a DCL text file to the other user by entering the FACSIMILE command. This command retrieves the text file and displays the text on both your terminal and the other user's terminal as if you had quickly typed all the text. (This, in effect, simulates the function of a FAX machine within the context of the PHONE utility).

In order to use this command, first press the PERCENT SIGN key to indicate that the next series of characters is a PHONE command. Enter the FACSIMILE command followed by the file specification of the text file you wish to transmit and finally press the RETURN key.

```
% FACSIMILE STATUS.REPORT
```

Once the document is displayed on the screen, you may continue to converse with the other user by entering additional text.

DIRECTORY

When using PHONE it is often useful to know the user name address of any users currently logged on to a particular VAX system. The DIRECTORY command displays all users currently logged in and whether or not they are available for a phone call or their phone is unplugged. (The last section within this chapter discusses unplugging the phone).

To obtain a listing of users on our own VAX system, simply enter the DIRECTORY command:

```
                    VAX/VMS Phone Facility              13-SEP-1989
%
Press any key to cancel the directory listing and continue.
--------------------------------------------------------------------
Process Name    User Name       Terminal        Phone Status

SMITH           SMITH           UTA4:           available
JONES           JONES           OPA0:           available

2 persons listed.
```

We may also get a similar listing for any other VAX to which we have access within the network. For example, to receive a listing of users on the VAX node name VAX1::, append the node name to the directory command as follows:

```
% DIRECTORY VAX1::
```

Note that the message displayed by the PHONE utility that states the display of users (which may include hundreds of users on large VAX systems and be quite lengthy) may be terminated by pressing any key.

Conference Calls

We may establish simultaneous PHONE sessions with multiple users, in effect a "conference call." With a conference call, the screen display of all users participating in the call includes a section for all other users in the call. Thus, any user may enter text that is then displayed in the appropriate screen section for all other users participating in the call.

To establish a conference call, place a call to the first user, as already discussed. Once that user has answered the call and a PHONE session is established, simply place another call to a second user as follows:

1) Press the PERCENT SIGN key to indicate to PHONE that the next series of characters is a command and not text to be displayed to the other user.

2) Place a call to the second user by simply entering the node name and user name address of the user.

3) Once the second user answers the call, the conference call is established.

Subsequent users may be included within the same call by following this same procedure. A total of eight users may simultaneously participate in the same call.

While you are conversing with one or more other users, you may also be called. Simply enter the ANSWER command, and a conference call will be established between you, the calling user, and the other users already included within the call.

Unplugging the Phone

We may wish to work for a time without interruption from any VAX PHONE calls; in effect, we wish to "unplug" our phone. This may be done simply by entering any of the following commands, already discussed in earlier chapters:

```
$ SET BROADCAST=(NOPHONE)

$ SET BROADCAST=(NONE)

$ SET TERMINAL/NOBROADCAST
```

Having entered these commands, we will no longer receive any ringing messages from users while we are at DCL level, and our phone will be listed as unavailable for any users performing the PHONE DIRECTORY command for our VAX system.

We may still enter the PHONE utility to place calls to other users. And if we are in the PHONE utility, the utility assumes that we may be willing to accept calls at this time and will display all ringing messages, which we may ANSWER or REJECT. Once we exit back to DCL, however, we will not receive any ringing messages and will be unavailable for incoming phone calls.

We may "plug" our phone back in and receive incoming calls with any of the following methods:

- Entering the command SET BROADCAST=(PHONE) or SET BROADCAST=(ALL).

- Entering the command SET TERMINAL/BROADCAST.

- Logging out and back in again. This resets our default to receive all broadcast messages, including PHONE and MAIL. (Unless, of course, our LOGIN.COM file sets our default to something different.)

HOLD

While we are engaged in a PHONE session with one or more users, we may place these users on hold. The other users are notified that we have currently placed them on hold. Meanwhile, we may enter any PHONE command, such as DIRECTORY, to obtain a listing of available users, or even DIAL or PHONE, to initiate another conversation with other users.

To place the other users in your current PHONE session on hold, enter the following command at the percent sign (%) prompt.

```
%   HOLD
```

UNHOLD

Once we have concluded a conversation with another user or group of users (with the HANGUP command), we may resume a conversation with users that we had placed on hold.

To resume a conversation that was placed on hold earlier, enter the following command:

```
%  UNHOLD
```

We may now resume our phone conversation with the users from our original PHONE session.

MAIL

It may be impossible for you to reach, via the PHONE utility, the user for whom you are looking. For instance, the user may not be logged in at the present time. Or, the user may be logged in but has refused all PHONE broadcast messages with the SET BROADCAST or SET TERMINAL/NOBROADCAST command.

Thus, from within the PHONE utility, we may wish to send a brief MAIL message to the other user. We may always send a MAIL message to another user even if all broadcast messages have been rejected or the user is not presently logged in.

At the percent sign prompt within the PHONE utility, we may enter the MAIL command, followed by the node name and user name address of the user we wish to send a mail message to, and a brief message.

```
%  MAIL EARTH::JONES "Please accept PHONE messages"
```

The brief message text is inserted within the SUBJECT portion of a mail message and the message is sent to the other user and inserted within his or her NEWMAIL folder.

Chapter 9 Exercises

Before attempting the exercises within this chapter for the MAIL and PHONE utilities, first obtain a few node names and user name addresses of others users with whom you can communicate.

As you can hopefully well appreciate after reading this chapter, the functions within MAIL are extensive. These exercises should be viewed only as a minimum series of steps. Once you have completed the exercises within the chapter, review the many command examples and screen snapshots within the chapter text and attempt additional functions on your own.

Exercise 1
Basic Functions

a)   Enter the MAIL utility from DCL by entering the MAIL command at the DCL prompt.

b)   At the MAIL prompt, enter the following basic commands:

   -   HELP to view the help text within the utility
   -   EXIT to terminate the mail session and return to DCL command level

Exercise 2
Sending Mail

a)   Using the EVE editor, create a text file named STATUS.REPORT.

b)   Mail the text file using the DCL command MAIL as follows:

```
$ MAIL STATUS.REPORT NODE::USER
```

c)   Send the message once again, this time using the qualifiers /SUBJECT, /PERSONAL_NAME, /SELF, and /CC.

d)   Enter the mail utility to create a message interactively by using the SEND or MAIL command from the MAIL prompt.

e) Set EVE as the editor of choice within MAIL by entering the SET EDITOR TPU command. Then create and send another message using the SEND/EDIT command.

f) Exit from the MAIL utility and return to DCL level. Using either the EVE editor or the DCL CREATE command, create a text file that contains a distribution list of mail addresses. Refer back to the sample distribution list within this chapter for the format and rules regarding such lists.

g) Begin another MAIL session. Send another MAIL message and use the distribution list just created for the mail addresses. Be sure to remember to use the @ symbol when specifying the file name of the distribution list file.

Exercise 3
Reading Mail

In order for you to perform the remaining exercises, you must, of course, have received some mail. If you have not received any mail from any other users, you may send yourself mail either by using the /SELF qualifier when you send mail to another user or by using your own node name and user name address in the TO portion of a message that you originate. (You are permitted to send mail to yourself in this manner).

a) Enter the DIRECTORY/FOLDERS command to note the existence of the NEWMAIL folder.

b) Enter the DIRECTORY NEWMAIL command to view a listing of the unread messages within the NEWMAIL folder.

c) Enter the READ/NEW command to view the first new message. Continue to press the RETURN key to read all messages, until you receive the "no more messages" notification.

d) Enter the DIRECTORY/FOLDERS and the DIRECTORY MAIL commands to note that the NEWMAIL folder is empty, as the messages that have just been read have been automatically moved into the MAIL folder.

Exercise 4
Scanning Through Messages

a) Select the MAIL folder with the DIRECTORY MAIL command.

b) Scan through the messages within the folder using the following commands:

- CURRENT
- BACK
- NEXT
- FIRST
- LAST

c) Return to the first message within the folder with the FIRST command. Then use the SEARCH command to search for the first occurrence of a string of text within one of the messages.

Exercise 5
Responding to Messages

a) Select the first message within the MAIL folder.

b) Reply to the sender of the message.

c) Select the second message within the MAIL folder.

d) Reply to the sender, using the selected editor.

e) Select the third message within the MAIL folder.

f) Forward the message to a third party.

Exercise 6
Folders

a) Select any message within any folder by entering the READ command.

b) Move the message out of the current folder and into a new folder named JANUARY. Answer Y to the prompt to create the new folder.

c) Select another message with the READ command.

d) Create a copy of the message in the same folder.

e) Use the DIRECTORY JANUARY command to view the new messages within the folder just created.

f) Select a message and copy the message to a new folder created in a subdirectory mail folder file.

Exercise 7
Deleting and Restoring Messages

a) Select the first message within the MAIL folder and delete.

b) View the MAIL folder to confirm the delete. View the WASTEBASKET folder to confirm that the message is being retained.

c) Select the message just deleted within the WASTEBASKET folder and move the message back into the original folder.

d) View both the MAIL and the WASTEBASKET folders to confirm that the message has been restored.

Exercise 8
Selecting Messages

a) Mark the first and third messages within the MAIL folder.

b) Select the marked messages within the same folder and view the listing of marked messages.

c) Copy only the selected messages into the folder JANUARY.

Exercise 9
MAIL Customization

Refer to the series of SET commands and customize the MAIL environment according to your preference. Use the corresponding SHOW commands, along with the SHOW ALL command to confirm the customization.

Exercise 10
MAIL Keypad

Refer to the MAIL keypad layout diagram. Attempt any desired functions by pressing the appropriate function key rather than entering the commands.

Exercise 11
PHONE

Once you have established a call with another user, any text that you type will be transmitted to the user you are conversing with. If you wish to enter a command, remember to first enter the percent sign (% or SHIFT 5) to indicate to PHONE that the next series of characters should not be transmitted to the other user but is a PHONE command.

a)   Place a call to another user.

b)   Answer a call from a user.

c)   Send a FAX document of a text file to the user.

d)   Obtain a directory listing of the users on your local VAX system.

e)   While conversing with another user, establish a conference call by calling a third user.

Exercise Answers

When performing the exercises or attempting to use the answers provided, watch carefully for which command level you are at. All answers within this section are assumed to be valid only for the MAIL command level (the MAIL> prompt), unless otherwise indicated. Other command levels are indicated by means of the dollar sign (for DCL commands) or the percent sign (for PHONE command level).

Exercise 1a-b

Self-explanatory

Exercise 2a

```
$ EDIT/TPU STATUS.REPORT
. . .
^ Z
```

Exercise 2b

Self-explanatory

Exercise 2c

```
$ MAIL                                 -
/SUBJECT="Sample subject"/SELF/CC      -
/PERSONAL_NAME="Sample name"           -
  STATUS.REPORT NODE::USER
```

Exercise 2d

Self-explanatory

Exercise 2e

Self-explanatory

Exercise 2f

```
$ CREATE SAMPLE.DIS
NODE1::USER1
NODE2::USER2
NODE3::USER3
^ Z
```

Exercise 2g

```
MAIL> SEND
To: @SAMPLE.DIS
```

Exercise 3a-d

Self-explanatory

Exercise 4a-c

Self-explanatory

Exercise 5a

```
READ MAIL 1
```

Exercise 5b

```
REPLY
```

Exercise 5c

```
SELECT MAIL
READ 2
```

Exercise 5d

```
REPLY/EDIT
```

Exercise 5e

```
SELECT MAIL
3
```

Exercise 5f

```
FORWARD
```

Exercise 6a

Self-explanatory

Exercise 6b

```
MOVE JANUARY
```

Exercise 6c

Self-explanatory

Exercise 6d

```
COPY JANUARY
```

Exercise 6e

Self-explanatory

Exercise 6f

```
$ CREATE/DIRECTORY [.MAIL]
$ MAIL
MAIL> READ MAIL 1
MAIL> COPY [.MAIL]NEWFOLDER.MAI
```

Exercise 7a

```
READ MAIL 1
DELETE
```

Exercise 7b

```
DIRECTORY/FOLDERS
DIRECTORY MAIL
DIRECTORY WASTEBASKET
```

Exercise 7c

```
READ WASTEBASKET 1
MOVE MAIL
```

Exercise 7d

```
DIRECTORY/FOLDERS
DIRECTORY MAIL
DIRECTORY WASTEBASKET
```

Exercise 8a

```
SELECT MAIL
MARK 1
MARK 3
```

Exercise 8b

```
SELECT/MARKED
DIRECTORY/MARKED
```

Exercise 8c

```
COPY/ALL JANUARY
```

Exercise 9

Self-explanatory

Exercise 10

Self-explanatory

Exercise 11a

```
$ PHONE NODE::USER
```

Exercise 11b

```
$ PHONE ANSWER
```

Exercise 11c

```
% FACSIMILE [SMITH]DAY1.MEMO
```

Exercise 11d

```
% DIAL NODE::USER
```

Appendix A

Glossary of Terms

Batch Job
A user job or procedure that executes in background mode. The advantage of batch jobs is that they can run concurrently with other user activity. See also "Log File."

CPU
Central Processing Unit. The device within the computer system which actually executes the program or software instructions. There are several ways of measuring the performance or capacity of a CPU, including the rating of the number of "millions of instructions per second" (MIPS) that a CPU can process.

There may be multiple CPUs within a single computer system to enhance the performance or MIPS capacity of a system.

DCL
Digital Command Language. DCL is the interface to the VMS operating system provided to the user.

DEC
Digital Equipment Corporation, the manufacturer of the VAX hardware and accompanying VMS operating system software.

Directory (see also Subdirectory, Directory Control File)
A portion of storage space on a disk drive allocated to a specific user or group of users. Access to files located within another individual's directory is generally restricted by means of system security.

Directory Control File
A file that contains information regarding the set up of a directory or subdirectory. Always contains a file name extension of .DIR. Not a text file that can be typed out by a user.

Disk
A hardware device used for storage of user files.

Disk block
A storage unit of 512 bytes or characters.

EDT
One of the two editors provided with the standard VMS operating system package.

Entry
A specific print or batch job number within a queue. The system automatically assigns entry numbers sequentially as users schedule print and batch jobs for execution.

Ethernet
A set of hardware and software products that permit VAX systems to communicate with other VAX systems and even non-VAX computers within a local area network.

EVE
Extensible VAX Editor. One of the two editors provided with the standard VMS operating system package.

LAN
Local area network. Digital's local area network strategy for VAX systems is Ethernet. The term is actually somewhat of a misnomer today, as current Ethernet technology permits VAX hosts to be interconnected within a LAN that is actually several milese.

Log File
A text file that contains the output from a batch job. A batch job is not associated with any user terminal, and thus requires a disk file to store the output for the job. See also "Batch Job."

Logical Name
A user-defined name for a VMS object, typically a file specification. The logical name may be used in place of the actual file specification.

Login
The process whereby a user can sign on to a VAX host computer by supplying a valid user identification name and corresponding password. A successful user login provides access to the Digital Command Language.

Logoff
Equivalent to logout.

Logon
Equivalent to login.

Logout
The process whereby the user signs off of a VAX host computer. Subsequent access to the VAX is available only after the user again logs in.

Node
In terms of computer networks, a computer system within the network. Within DECnet networks, a node is identified to users with an alphabetic name no more than six characters in length.

Operating System
Software supplied by the computer hardware manufacturer which provides the user with an interface to the hardware system. Not to be confused with user-written or purchased application software.

Operator
One or more individuals within the computer room who physically monitor the computer system. Typical operator duties include start up and shut down of the computer system, mounting magnetic tape reels and disk storage packs for users, maintaining printer functioning, etc.

PID
Process Identification. A randomly generated number automatically determined by VMS and assigned to every process at the time of process creation. No two processes have the same PID number. Therefore, the PID is used to uniquely identify a process.

Print Job
A text file submitted to one of the available print queues for printing when the associated print device is available.

Process
A job currently executing on the system. In addition to interactive processes for user sessions, there are also system processes, batch processes, user subprocesses and others.

Queue
Either a print or a batch queue. Queues sequentially service a print job for printing on an output device or a batch job for execution on a VAX host.

Session
The period of activity for an interactive user from the time they first login until the log out. Thus, a user may have either one or several sessions throughout a workday.

Subdirectory
Subsidiary directories within an individual's main directory. Subdirectories are created in a hierarchical manner and provide smaller, more convenient subgroupings of files than a single main directory.

Symbol
For DCL users, a symbol permits definition of a user command, that is, an alias name or symbol for a DCL command verb and possibly optional qualifiers. Several additional uses of symbols are permitted within VMS.

System Manager
One or more individuals within the computer data center concerned with the technical configuration and troubleshooting of the computer system environment. Typical system management duties include installation of computer software, problem resolution, creation of user accounts, etc.

Terminal
A hardware device that provides the user interface to a computer system.

Terminal Server
Within an Ethernet environment, the terminal server provides the user terminal with access to the Ethernet network and, therefore, the VAX and non-VAX hosts connected to the Ethernet.

Text File
A user data file that contains alphanumeric text, as opposed to binary data. Typically, text files are created and maintained by users with editors.

UIC
User Identification Code. A security code assigned by the system manager for each user authorized for the system. The UIC is comprised of both a group code and an individual code and serves both to identify a specific user and to classify that user along with others within a group. The UIC determines a user's access to files and other system resources.

User
Technically, any individual who uses the computer system. Its use within this textbook is to identify a general DCL user, as distinguished from an operator or system manager.

VAX
Virtual Address Extension. The name of a line of computer hardware systems manufactured by Digital Equipment Corporation.

Verb
A DCL command or that part of a command sentence which specifies *what* the user wishes to do. A foreign command or verb may be defined by the user using a symbol.

VMS
Virtual Memory System. The operating system software supplied by Digital Equipment Corporation to run on the VAX hardware.

Appendix B

Summary of DCL Commands

@	Invokes a DCL command procedure.
=	Assigns a DCL command string to a local symbol or foreign command. Use a double equal sign (==) to define a global symbol.
APPEND	Appends the contents of one file to the end of another file.
COPY	Copies the contents of one file into another file.
CREATE	Creates a text file. Only line editing features are available. The creation is terminated with the CONTROL Z key.
CREATE/DIRECTORY	Creates a main-level directory or subdirectory. Special privileges are usually required to create a main-level directory, while none are required to create a subdirectory.
DEASSIGN	Deletes a logical name that has been defined with the DEFINE command.
DEFINE	Defines a logical name that usually equates to a physical file specification or a portion of a physical file specification.
DELETE	Deletes a file from the disk.
DELETE/ENTRY	Deletes a batch or print job (entry) from a queue.
DELETE/SYMBOL	Deletes a local symbol defined with the equal sign (=). To delete a global symbol, use the /GLOBAL qualifier. To delete all symbols, whether local or global, also use the /ALL qualifier.
DIRECTORY	Generates a listing of the files within a directory or subdirectory. Numerous qualifiers exist to display detailed information regarding the files listed.

EDIT/EDT	Invokes the EDT editor.
EDIT/TPU	Invokes the EVE editor.
HELP	Invokes the VMS HELP utility.
LOGOUT	Terminates the current DCL process and logs the user off of the VAX.
MAIL	Invokes the VAX MAIL utility.
PRINT	Submits a text file to one of the print queues for printing. Various qualifiers exist to control the specific processing of the print job or entry.
PHONE	Invokes the VAX PHONE utility.
PURGE	Deletes all older versions of a file.
RECALL	Recalls up to 20 of the most recent DCL commands entered within the current DCL session.
RENAME	Changes the name of a file from an original name to a new name.
SET BROADCAST	Allows the user to reject or accept broadcast messages from various utilities.
SET CONTROL	Sets on or off the CONTROL Y (process interrupt) or the CONTROL T (process status) functions of DCL.
SET DEFAULT	Changes the default directory assumed by DCL when no specific directory is included within a file specification.
SET DIRECTORY/ VERSION_LIMIT	Changes the version limit assigned to new files subsequently created within the directory or subdirectory named. Initially, a virtually infinite number of versions are retained.

SET ENTRY	Changes the specific attributes of a print entry or batch entry within one of the queues.
SET FILE/ ERASE_ON_DELETE	Sets the ERASE option as the automatic procedure to be performed for a file whenever the file is deleted with either the DELETE or PURGE commands.
SET FILE/ OWNER_UIC	Changes the owner UIC attached to a file. Initially, a file receives the UIC of the process that first creates the file.
SET FILE/ PROTECTION	Changes the protection codes assigned to a file. Initially, files receive the default protection codes stated with the SET PROTECTION command.
SET FILE/ VERSION_LIMIT	Changes the number of versions retained for an existing file. Initially, the file will retain the number of versions specified with the SET DIRECTORY/VERSION_LIMIT command at the time the file was created.
SET PASSWORD	Changes the password for the current user name. The user name and password combination are required at the time of login.
SET PROCESS/NAME	Changes the name assigned to the process. Initially, the process name is assigned the same name as either the user name or the terminal number.
SET PROMPT	Changes the DCL prompt. Initially, the default DCL prompt is the dollar sign ($).
SET PROTECTION/ DEFAULT	Changes the default protection code to be assigned to new files created by the process.
SET TERMINAL	Changes various terminal characteristics.
SHOW BROADCAST	Displays the messages accepted or rejected as specified by the SET BROADCAST command.

SHOW ENTRY | Displays the attributes for one or more print or batch job entries within the queues. Such entries are created with the PRINT (print jobs) or SUBMIT (batch jobs) command.

SHOW LOGICAL | Displays the physical definition of one or more logical names.

SHOW PROCESS | Displays the characteristics of a DCL process.

SHOW PROTECTION | Displays the default protection code to be assigned new files created by the process, as stated with the SET PROTECTION/DEFAULT command.

SHOW QUEUE | Displays the print and batch queues on the system, along with any entries we may have within the queues.

SHOW QUOTA | Displays the quota of disk blocks that the user is limited to using.

SHOW SYMBOL | Displays the definition of a local symbol or foreign command. Use the /GLOBAL qualifier for global symbols. Also, use the /ALL qualifier to display the definitions for all local or global symbols.

SHOW SYSTEM | Displays the current list of processes, including system, batch, interactive and subprocesses, currently active within the system.

SHOW TIME | Displays the current system date and time.

SHOW USERS | Displays the current list of interactive processes.

SUBMIT | Submits a command procedure file as a batch job entry to be processed within one of the queues.

TYPE   Types out the contents of a text file on the
                              terminal screen.

Appendix C

Summary of EVE Editor Commands

BOTTOM	Moves the cursor to the bottom of the document.
BUFFER	Changes the buffer currently displayed.
CAPITALIZE WORD	Capitalizes the first letter of the current word or the words selected and highlighted.
CENTER LINE	Centers the current line or the lines selected and highlighted according to the current margins.
COPY	Copies the text currently selected and highlighted to a buffer. Text within the buffer may later be inserted in another position.
DCL	Allows the execution of any DCL command with the output appearing in a read-only buffer named DCL.
DEFINE KEY	Allows function keys to be defined by the user as equivalents for any EVE command.
DELETE BUFFER	Deletes a buffer currently loaded within the EVE session.
ENLARGE WINDOW	Enlarges the current screen window by the number of lines indicated.
ERASE CHARACTER	Erases the current character or the characters selected and highlighted.
ERASE LINE	Erases the current line.
ERASE PREVIOUS WORD	Erases the word before the current cursor position.
ERASE START OF LINE	Erases from the current cursor position to the start of the line.
ERASE WORD	Erases the current word.

EXIT	Terminates the EVE session, saves the contents of the current buffer to a disk file, and returns the user to DCL command level.
FILL	Justifies the text at the current paragraph or the text selected and highlighted.
FIND	Allows the entry of text and begins a search for the text.
GET FILE	Loads a file into a new and unique buffer for editing.
INCLUDE FILE	Loads or includes a file into an existing buffer already associated with another file. Does not alter the file being loaded or included.
INSERT HERE	Inserts the text currently located within the "cut" buffer into the current cursor position.
INSERT PAGE	Inserts a page break character at the current cursor position.
LOWERCASE WORD	Changes all the characters within the current word or the words selected and highlighted, to lowercase characters.
MOVE BY LINE	Moves the cursor one line forward/reverse.
MOVE BY PAGE	Moves the cursor one page forward/reverse.
MOVE BY WORD	Moves the cursor one word forward/reverse.
NEXT SCREEN	Moves the cursor one screen section forward.
NEXT WINDOW	Moves the cursor to the next window on the screen.
ONE WINDOW	Removes the display of all EVE windows on the screen with the exception of the current window.

PREVIOUS SCREEN	Moves the cursor one screen section back.
PREVIOUS WINDOW	Moves the cursor to the previous window on the screen.
REMOVE	Removes or "cuts" the text selected and highlighted and replaces any text currently stored within the "cut" buffer.
REPLACE	Removes the text selected and highlighted and replaces the text with the current contents of the "cut" buffer.
RESET	Removes any select mark currently in effect.
RESTORE	Restores the text most recently erased.
RESTORE CHARACTER	Restores the character most recently erased.
RESTORE LINE	Restores the line most recently erased.
RESTORE WORD	Restores the word most recently erased
SELECT	Marks the beginning of a select region of text. Subsequent cursor movement keys will highlight the text selected.
SET CURSOR BOUND	Sets the cursor mode to bound. A bound cursor can only move to locations on the screen where text has already been entered.
SET CURSOR FREE	Sets the cursor mode to free. A free cursor can move to any location on the screen. When the cursor is moved to a location after the end of a line or the end of the document and text is then inserted, EVE automatically pads the text with the necessary spaces or lines.
SET KEYPAD EDT SET KEYPAD NOEDT	Turns on or off EVE's emulation of the EDT function keypad, which uses the terminal numeric keypad.

SET LEFT MARGIN	Sets the left margin to the column indicated.
SET RIGHT MARGIN	Sets the right margin to the column indicated.
SET WIDTH	Sets the width of the screen display to the number of characters indicated.
SET WRAP SET NOWRAP	Turns on or off wrapping of words to the next line when the word is entered beyond the right margin column.
SHIFT LEFT	Shifts the view of the screen display to the left by the number of characters indicated.
SHIFT RIGHT	Shifts the view of the screen display to the right by the number of characters indicated.
SHOW BUFFERS	Displays all buffers currently active for the EVE session.
SHRINK WINDOW	Shrinks the current EVE window by the number of lines indicated.
SPLIT WINDOW	Splits the current EVE window into the number of additional windows indicated.
TOP	Moves the cursor to the top of the document.
TWO WINDOWS	Splits the current EVE window into one additional window or two windows.
UPPERCASE WORD	Changes all the characters within the current word, or the words selected and highlighted, to uppercase characters.
WRITE FILE	Writes the contents of the current buffer to the disk file indicated.

Appendix D

Summary of MAIL Utility Commands

ANSWER	Creates an answer to a mail message. Synonymous with REPLY.
BACK	Moves back one message within the current folder.
COMPRESS	Compresses and reconstructs the MAIL file, removing any wasted space as a result of maintenance to messages.
COPY	Copies the current message into the folder indicated.
CURRENT	Moves to the beginning of the current message.
DELETE	Deletes the current message or the set of messages indicated. Actually performs a MOVE to the WASTEBASKET folder.
DIRECTORY	Displays the messages within the current folder or the folder indicated.
EXIT	Terminates the MAIL session and returns the user to DCL command level. Any messages within the wastebasket are automatically deleted.
EXTRACT	Copies the current message to the DCL text file indicated.
FILE	Moves the current message out of the current folder and into the folder indicated. Synonymous with MOVE.
FIRST	Moves to the first message within the current folder.
LAST	Moves to the last message within the current folder.

MAIL	Sends a message to another user. Synonymous with SEND.
MARK UNMARK	Marks or unmarks the current message or the set of messages indicated.
MOVE	Moves the current message out of the current folder and into the folder indicated. Synonymous with FILE.
NEXT	Moves to the next message within the current folder.
PRINT	Adds the current message to the set of messages to be queued for printing when the current MAIL session terminates.
PURGE	Immediately deletes all messages being retained within the WASTEBASKET folder.
QUIT	Terminates the mail session and returns the user to DCL command level without deleting messages being retained within the wastebasket.
READ	Reads the message indicated.
READ/NEW	Reads the first message within the NEWMAIL folder.
REPLY	Creates an answer to a mail message. Synonymous with ANSWER.
SEARCH	Searches for the first message within the current folder that contains the text indicated, or simply searches for the next message within the current folder that contains the text previously indicated.
SELECT	Selects all messages within the folder indicated. Synonymous with SET FOLDER.

SELECT/BEFORE	Selects those messages received before the date indicated from the folder indicated.
SELECT/CC	Selects those messages within the folder indicated that contain the node name and user name address indicated within the CC list portion of the message header.
SELECT/FROM	Selects those messages within the folder indicated that contain the node name and user name address indicated within the FROM portion of the message header.
SELECT/MARKED	Selects those messages within the folder indicated that have been marked.
SELECT/SINCE	Selects those messages received since the date indicated from the folder indicated.
SELECT/SUBJECT	Selects those messages within the folder indicated that contain the text indicated within the SUBJECT portion of the message header.
SEND	Sends a message to another user. Synonymous with MAIL.
SET AUTO_PURGE SET NOAUTO_PURGE	Turns on or off the automatic purge or deletion of messages being retained within the wastebasket.
SET CC SET NOCC	Sets on or off the automatic prompting of node name and user name addresses to be included within a message CC list.
SET COPY_SELF SEND SET COPY_SELF NOSEND	Sets on or off the automatic creation of a copy to oneself of any messages sent via the SEND or MAIL commands.
SET COPY_SELF REPLY SET COPY_SELF NOREPLY	Sets on or off the automatic creation of a copy to oneself of any messages sent via the REPLY or ANSWER commands.

SET COPY_SELF FORWARD SET COPY_SELF NOFORWARD	Sets on or off the automatic creation of a copy to oneself of any messages sent via the FORWARD command.
SET EDITOR	Uses the editor indicated as the editor to be called whenever the /EDIT qualifier is used when creating a message with the SEND or MAIL, REPLY or ANSWER, or FORWARD commands.
SET FOLDER	Selects all messages within the folder indicated. Synonymous with SELECT. All qualifiers of the SET FOLDER command are likewise synonymous with SELECT.
SET FORWARD SET NOFORWARD	Sets or erases a forwarding node name and user name address to which all mail received is automatically forwarded.
SET MAIL_DIRECTORY	Sets a MAIL directory other than the initial default of the user's top level directory, as indicated by the SYS$LOGIN logical name.
SET PERSONAL_NAME SET NOPERSONAL_NAME	Sets or erases a personalized return address to be appended to the standard node name and user name return address for any outgoing messages.
SET QUEUE	Sets a default queue for the MAIL PRINT command other than the initial default of SYS$PRINT. Has no effect on the defaults for the DCL PRINT command.
SET WASTEBASKET_NAME	Specifies a folder name for the wastebasket folder other than the default name of WASTEBASKET.

SHOW ALL	Displays the current settings of all MAIL customization options available to users with the various SET commands.
SHOW AUTO_PURGE	Displays whether or not an automatic purge of the WASTEBASKET folder is performed when the MAIL session is terminated with the EXIT command.
SHOW CC	Displays whether or not a CC list is prompted whenever an outgoing message is created.
SHOW COPY_SELF	Displays whether or not an automatic copy of any outgoing messages are sent to oneself when using the MAIL or SEND, ANSWER or REPLY, or FORWARD command.
SHOW EDITOR	Displays the editor to be called whenever the /EDIT qualifier is used when creating a message with the SEND or MAIL, REPLY or ANSWER, or FORWARD commands.
SHOW FOLDER	Displays the current default folder.
SHOW FORWARD	Displays whether or not any node name and user name forwarding address has been specified for the MAIL account.
SHOW MAIL_DIRECTORY	Displays the current default MAIL disk directory.
SHOW PERSONAL_NAME	Displays whether or not a personalized return address message is appended to the default node name and user name address of the sending user.
SHOW QUEUE	Displays the default queue name assumed by the MAIL PRINT command.

SHOW WASTEBASKET_NAME   Displays   the   name   of   the
                          WASTEBASKET folder.

Appendix E

Summary of
PHONE Utility Commands

ANSWER	Answers an incoming phone call placed by another user.
DIAL	Dials another user. Synonymous with PHONE.
DIRECTORY	Displays a listing of all users currently logged on to the VAX system indicated with the command. Also displays whether the users listed are available or not for incoming phone calls.
EXIT	Synonymous with CONTROL Z. Exits from the PHONE utility back to DCL command level.
FACSIMILE	Roughly simulates the function of a FAX machine by including a DCL text file within a PHONE session. The text file indicated with the FACSIMILE command is displayed on the user's screen as if the originating user had typed the text directly.
HANGUP	Ends a phone call currently under way with another user.
HOLD	Places all current calls on hold.
PHONE	Dials another user. Synonymous with DIAL.
REJECT	Rejects an incoming phone call from another user. Incoming phone calls are indicated by repeated "ringing" messages generated by the calling user.
UNHOLD	Takes off of hold all users placed on hold with the most recent HOLD command.

Appendix F

EDT Synopsis

The EDT editor is the older of the two editors between EDT and EVE. It is also the default editor invoked with the DCL EDIT command.

The editor has three basic modes:

- Line editing mode
- Full-screen (change) mode
- Command mode

Full-screen mode is the most useful since it is within this mode that the EDT function keypad discussed earlier is active. The functions available with this keypad are almost identical to the EVE emulation of the EDT keypad already discussed.

The EDT editor is invoked with the /EDT qualifier of the EDIT command, or with the EDIT command itself (/EDT is the default), as follows:

```
$ EDIT/EDT

    or

$ EDIT
```

When entering the EDIT/EDT command, the name of an existing file to be modified or a new file to be created must be supplied. If the required file name parameter is not supplied, the command automatically prompts the user for one. Note the following example:

```
$ EDIT/EDT
_File: FILE1.MEMO
*
```

The asterisk indicates that the user is currently at EDT line editing mode. There are numerous line editing commands available within this mode of the editor and described within the documentation provided by DEC. We will mention only the following commands at line editing mode:

- C or SET MODE CHANGE, to leave line editing mode and enter full screen mode and use the EDT function keypad.

- EXIT, to end the editing session and return to DCL level. Any modifications made during the session are written to the disk file indicated.

- QUIT, to end the editing session and return to DCL level. Any modifications made during the session are not written to the disk file and the changes are ignored.

Once full screen mode has been selected, the following functions are available:

- CONTROL Z to exit full-screen mode and return to line editing mode and the asterisk (*) prompt.

- The EDT function keypad.

- The ARROW function keys of LEFT ARROW, RIGHT ARROW, UP ARROW and DOWN ARROW. The GOLD ARROW combinations discussed within EVE are not available.

- The editing keypad functions, namely FIND, INSERT HERE, REMOVE, SELECT, PREV SCREEN and NEXT SCREEN. Their function within EDT is almost identical to that described for EVE.

- EDT command mode, by pressing the GOLD 7 key. (Within EVE, the GOLD 7 key combination produces EVE command mode. However, within the EDT editor, EDT command mode is provided).

Documentation regarding the EDT command mode is provided within the documentation provided by DEC.

Note

Little information is provided herein for the EDT editor, despite its familiarity to many long-time VAX/VMS users. This is for two reasons: (1) the aforementioned benefits of EVE, (2) the EVE emulation of the EDT keypad, and (3) the fact that some question now exists as to whether the EDT editor will even be available within future versions of the VMS operating system. The fact that support for the EDT editor may be dropped at some future date appears quite plausible given the fact that emulation of the EDT keypad is now available within the EVE editor.

Users who wish to use the EDT editor may do so by entering EDT full-screen mode as follows, and thereafter using the EDT function keypad, the ARROW keys and the editing keypad, as discussed within the chapter on the EVE editor.

```
$ EDIT/EDT FILE1.MEMO
*   C
```

Following the completion of the edits, terminate the EDT session as follows:

- Press CONTROL Z to exit full-screen mode and return to line editing mode and the asterisk prompt.

- At line editing mode, enter either the EXIT command to save the edits or QUIT to ignore the edits, and return to DCL command level.

References

For a complete description of the VAX/VMS operating system, including the DCL interface, consult the following reference manuals available from Digital Equipment Corporation.

Using VMS, Guide to Using VMS
General User, DCL Dictionary
Using VMS, MAIL, PHONE
Processing Text, EVE Reference
Processing Text, EDT Reference

Index